FIGHTER

FIGHTER

Chris Chant
Illustrated by John Batchelor

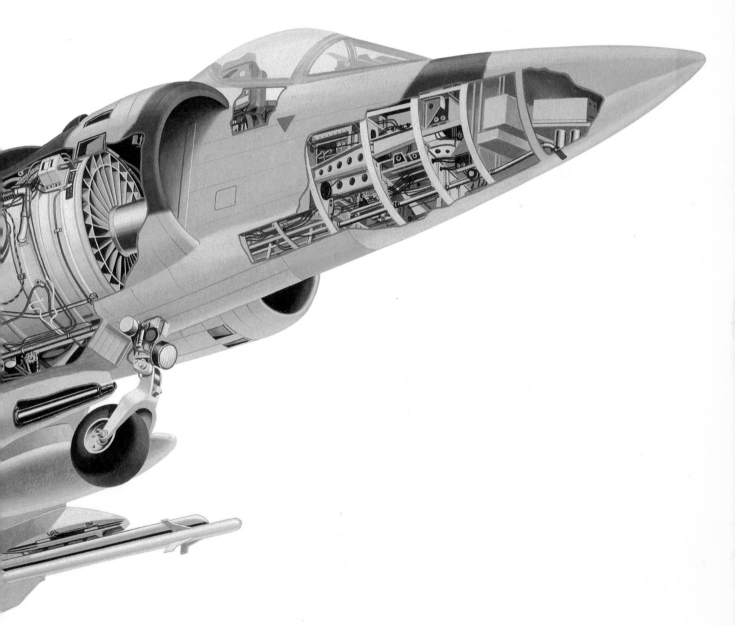

A David & Charles Military Book

British Library Cataloguing in Publication Data

Batchelor, John, *1936–*
  Fighter. – (A David & Charles military
  book).
  1. Fighter planes – History
  I. Title   II. Chant, Christopher
  623.74′64′09   UG1242.F5

  ISBN 0-7153-9171-2

Printed in Portugal
for David & Charles Publishers plc
Brunel House   Newton Abbot   Devon

Distributed in the United States of America
Sterling Publishing Co., Inc.
2 Park Ave., New York, NY10016

Design by Graham Beehag
Photo research by Military Archive & Research Services

CONTENTS

INTRODUCTION

Today's fighter is a wonder of structural and electronic engineering made possible by the skills of the aerodynamicist, systems designer, engine manufacturer and a veritable host of others. All the objective skills and subjective intuitions of these men are blended into the blueprints (or more recently the magnetic tracks in a computer's memory) for the combat aeroplane we call the fighter, and then turned into hardware by skilled workers, taken on their first flights by test pilots, evaluated by service experts, improved as necessary, and finally ordered into mass production for service use. And this is only the start of the story, for in service the fighter is constantly monitored, maintained, refurbished, upgraded and at times virtually rebuilt to keep it right up to the mark.

Yet the same account can be given of every fighter ever built: earlier fighters may have lacked the sophistication of modern types, but they went through the same processes, and reflected the cutting edge of contemporary aeronautical technologies in just the same way that the modern fighter exemplifies its 'state-of-the-art' characteristics.

This is the case because in essence the fighter has changed little in concept in the three-quarters of a century since the first rudimentary fighters and their inexperienced pilots took off to create the new science of air combat. So there is a common link running through the story of the fighter: for 75 years the fighter's task has been to prevent the enemy's aircraft from going about their intended purposes: bombers shot down preferably before they have been able to unload their weapons on the designated ground target, reconnaissance aircraft prevented from returning home with invaluable photographic (or in later years electronic) intelligence, close support aircraft despatched before they have been able to aid their ground forces, and fighters destroyed before they have been able to intervene in a similar fashion for the other side.

Throughout this process these have been constants and, together with the basic role, it is these that mark the fighter for what it is. The relative importance attached to the various components of the 'fighter equation' has fluctuated with the fashions and tactical doctrines of the day, but among the key components are speed, acceleration, rate of climb, rate of turn, overall agility, a good field of vision for the pilot, effective armament and, least definable of all, the harmonious blending of these components into a complete unit that functions as an integrated machine under the direct control of the pilot.

The fighter has evolved along these lines, and it is a story of

abiding fascination for all interested in air warfare and technical history. The predominant country has shifted with period, there have been eras of slow progress, and there have been times when fighters seem to have been developed pellmell. The story is too large for a small volume such as this, so the emphasis throughout has been placed on sketching the basic pattern of development, and then illustrating these patterns with the fighters that created, modified or at times broke them, and so started the process towards a new variant on the same fighter theme.

It is hoped that the reader can appreciate and grasp the main tactical and technical trends, which are discussed in this book in terms of the original production version of the fighter unless otherwise specified. The further development of in-service types has only been outlined in this treatment where relevant to the development of the fighter as such. It is hoped, therefore, that the very limited amount of hard technical information that can be packed into so small a compass satisfies, at least to a modest degree, the reader's appetite for information about that most important and colourful instrument of aerial warfare – the fighter.

1915-1935
The Biplane Era

Fighter – the word fully describes the task of one of the most important combat aircraft types in any air force's inventory. Some might disagree with the assertion that the fighter is a significant type, for its function is essentially defensive: in offensive air operations it secures air superiority so that other first-line aircraft can go about their business without hindrance from the enemy, while in defensive operations it seeks to prevent the enemy's aircraft from fulfilling their own primary tasks. The fighter can thus be regarded as a spoiler of the enemy's air intentions, and is therefore a key weapon in its own right. Over the years the qualities that go to making a fighter have been altered and at times blurred by the need of the fighter to undertake a number of secondary tasks (most notably close support of friendly ground forces in and after World War II), but the salient features and characteristics remain as valid today as they did some 70 years ago, when the first true fighters began to appear.

The fighter began to emerge as a weapon in its own right during World War I, but even before this far-sighted men had begun to appreciate that the aeroplane could be more than just a toy that might perhaps be used for reconnaissance, or scouting as it was called at the time. These early visionaries were in reality looking well ahead of the aircraft capabilities of the day, for heavier-than-air craft in the first 10 years of their existence were strictly limited in capabilities by the low power of their engines and their flimsy structures, which both served to curtail performance and load-carrying capability.

The U.S. Army had issued the world's first specification for a military aeroplane in 1907, resulting in the Wright A (Fort Myer), but it was not until 1910 that the first armament experiments were carried out. In June of that year the American pioneer Glenn Curtiss used one of his own biplanes to drop dummy bombs on the outline of a battleship marked in the water by buoys. But of greater significance for the evolution of the fighter was the world's first known use of a gun from an aeroplane in August 1910 when another American, Jacob Fickel, fired a rifle at a ground target. This was an extremely precarious act despite the limited recoil of the single-shot rifle, for seat belts and any real support for the firer were totally lacking from the aircraft of the day. More precarious still, but of greater long-term importance, was the world's first use of a machine-gun from an aeroplane in June 1912, when Captain Charles de Forest Chandler of the U.S. Army fired a Lewis light machine-

gun from a completely exposed position on the lower wing of a Wright B biplane flown by another army officer. Thereafter experiments followed with fair speed, another significant moment occurring in July 1913 when a 37-mm Coventry Ordnance Works cannon was fired in the air for the first time. For its time this weapon offered a prodigious capability, and the weapon is of great historical interest as it operated on the recoilless principle, being designed to fire a large-calibre projectile whose recoil was balanced by the firing of an equal mass of lead shot in the opposite direction: this reduced the loads on the aeroplane's structure to virtually nil, but meant of course that the weapon had to be aimed in a direction in which neither the projectile nor the counter-mass would hit the aeroplane!

By the time the Coventry Ordnance Works' cannon was being tested, the world had seen the first use of aircraft in war, when the Italians used a small number of miscellaneous machines during their conquest of Tripolitania from the Turks in 1911-12. The Italians restricted themselves to reconnaissance at first, but the path ahead was foreshadowed when they started to use extemporised bombs to attack Turkish positions. Needless to say, the future was foreshadowed yet further by the inevitable response by the Turks,

Above: The Gloster Gamecock was typical of biplane fighter design and structure in the 1920s. Introduced in 1926, this was the Royal Air Force's last biplane fighter of wooden construction, and featured the standard twin-gun armament and open cockpit.

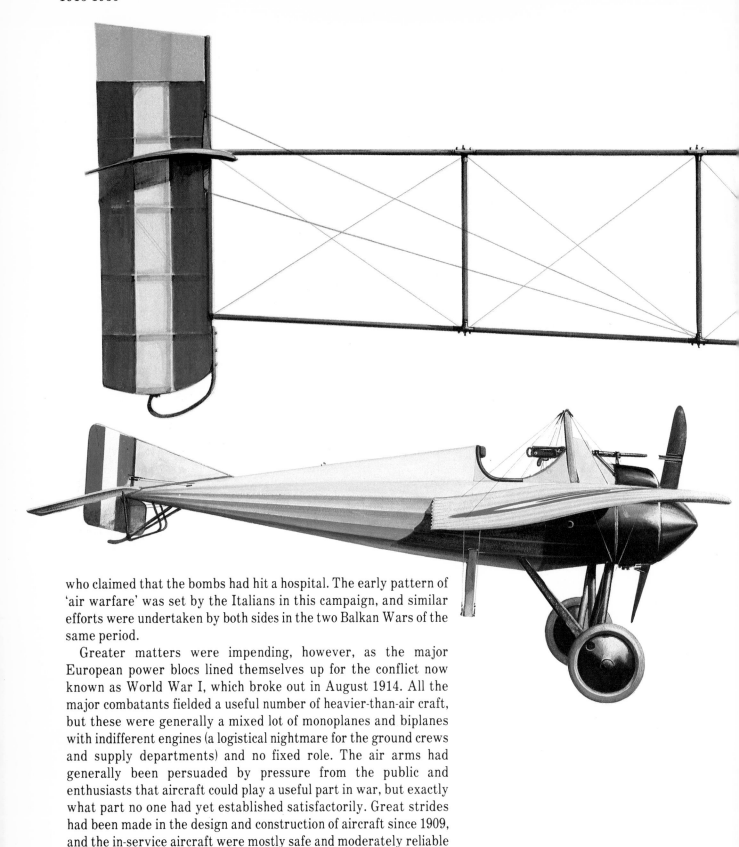

who claimed that the bombs had hit a hospital. The early pattern of 'air warfare' was set by the Italians in this campaign, and similar efforts were undertaken by both sides in the two Balkan Wars of the same period.

Greater matters were impending, however, as the major European power blocs lined themselves up for the conflict now known as World War I, which broke out in August 1914. All the major combatants fielded a useful number of heavier-than-air craft, but these were generally a mixed lot of monoplanes and biplanes with indifferent engines (a logistical nightmare for the ground crews and supply departments) and no fixed role. The air arms had generally been persuaded by pressure from the public and enthusiasts that aircraft could play a useful part in war, but exactly what part no one had yet established satisfactorily. Great strides had been made in the design and construction of aircraft since 1909, and the in-service aircraft were mostly safe and moderately reliable within their limitations, but as yet lacked the ability to carry much of a useful load other than the pilot and, in some machines, one passenger. The role of such aircraft had perforce to be purely optical

Below: The Voisin Type 5 (LA.S) was primarily a bomber with 150-hp (1120-kW) Salmson (Canton-Unné) engine, but its armament of one 8-mm (0.315-in) Hotchkiss machine-gun gave it modest offensive capability. Speed was a stately 65 mph (105 km/h).

Left: Developed in 1913, the Morane-Saulnier Type N was a high-speed scout with an 80-hp (60-kW) rotary. The type was also used as an interim fighter in 1915-16 with a fixed Hotchkiss or Vickers gun and deflector plates on the propeller blades.

reconnaissance, with the aircraft despatched whenever the weather permitted to scout the enemy's front line and, in the absence of radio communication, return to base before reporting enemy movements and concentrations. The task was made easier by the fact that ground camouflage against aerial reconnaissance was non-existent, and anti-aircraft fire was restricted to individuals with the enthusiasm to use their small arms against any aerial intruders, generally without regard for side.

It is not surprising, therefore, that useful information began to accrue from this limited effort. The most notable result of the reconnaissance effort in the opening stages of World War I was the British and French detection of the German left-wheel towards Paris, allowing the Allied withdrawal that led to the decisive 1st Battle of the Marne. This halted the Germans' initial offensive, and led to 'The Race to the Sea' as each side sought to outflank the other with a northward extension of its line. The result was the establishment of the front line from the coast of the English Channel to the Franco-Swiss border that was to remain essentially unchanged but increasingly fortified for most of World War I.

Early air operations had thus proved that reconnaissance could play a useful part in the overall scheme of operations. It thus became clear to each side that if the enemy could profit from air reconnaissance, it would be useful to prevent him from securing such an advantage. There was initially great enthusiasm for the development of anti-aircraft guns in response to this 'threat', but though these deterred the enemy and forced him to operate at greater altitude, they were not on their own cost-effective: what was needed was an aeroplane type that could match the performance of the enemy's unarmed or lightly armed reconnaissance aircraft and use a weapon to bring it down. As we have seen, several experiments had been conducted before World War I, and considerable thought had been exercised towards the development of genuinely effective armament systems for aircraft, but none of these had borne any practical fruit by 1914 or, indeed, early 1915.

Yet the more adventurous pilots had already begun to make their own individual efforts, and many a miscellaneous weapon had been taken aloft in the hope of engaging the enemy. Some of these schemes were wild in the extreme, being characterised at best by an excess of enthusiasm and at worst by foolhardiness: typical of such efforts were a grapnel on the end of a rope, which the pilot might

Right: **Introduced in 1917 in useful numbers, the Morane-Saulnier Type AI was a parasol-wing fighter with a single synchronised Vickers gun and a speed of 130 mph (210 km/h) on its 160-hp (119-kW) Le Rhône rotary.**

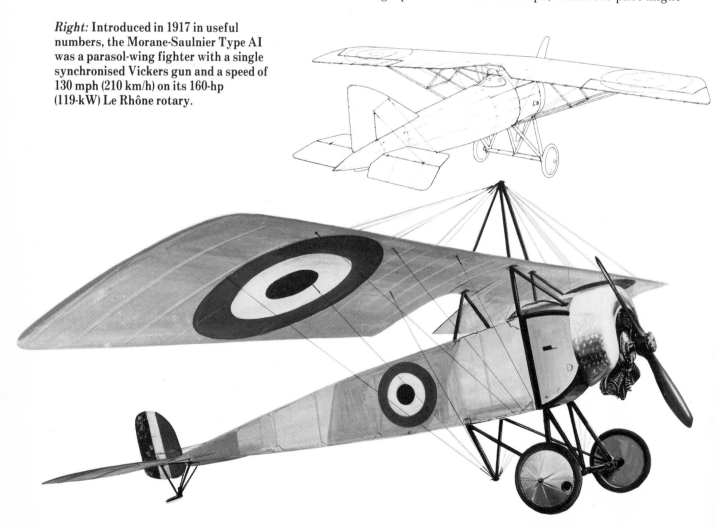

Right: **The Bristol M.1C, otherwise known as the Bullet, failed because of specious technical opposition, so costing the Royal Flying Corps a potentially decisive fighter for service on the Western Front. This three-view illustration highlights the Bullet's exceptional lines, allowing it to reach 130 mph (209 km/h) on its 110-hp (82-kW) Le Rhône rotary.**

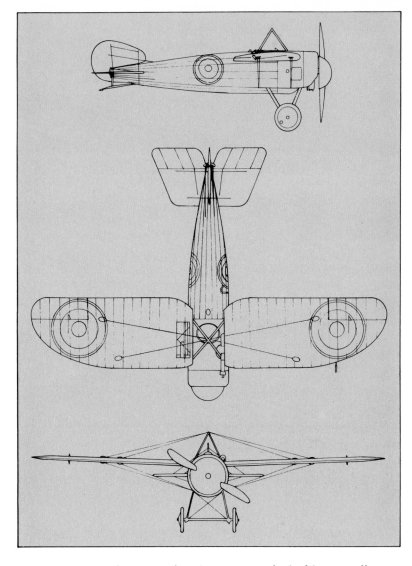

Below left: **The Morane-Saulnier Type L was designed in 1913 and used in the early part of World War I as a scout. The parasol wing offered good fields of vision, and the aeroplane became the world's first 'fighter' when fitted with a machine-gun and deflector plates.**

use to tear up the enemy's wings or tangle in his propeller, or grenades which the pilot hoped he might be able to drop onto an enemy aeroplane flying below his own machine. The favourites were more realistic weapons such as rifles, carbines and pistols, which were all comparatively light and sufficiently handy for use in the confined volume of an aeroplane's cockpit: some successes were scored, but for the most part these were attributable to luck as much as skill, because the problems of firing accurately from one machine manoeuvring in two and possibly three dimensions against a target manoeuvring in similar fashion were and of course remain enormous, and had in 1914-15 hardly even been addressed.

Yet a decisive occasion had been recorded on 5 October 1914 when a German Aviatik biplane was brought down by the fire of a Hotchkiss machine-gun carried in a French aeroplane, a Voisin pusher biplane flown by Sergeant Joseph Frantz. This marked a new departure for the history of air warfare, signalling the advent of the era in which it was increasingly realized that volumes of aimed fire rather than individual aimed shots were needed for air-to-air combat. This episode was very much a lone example, but if any

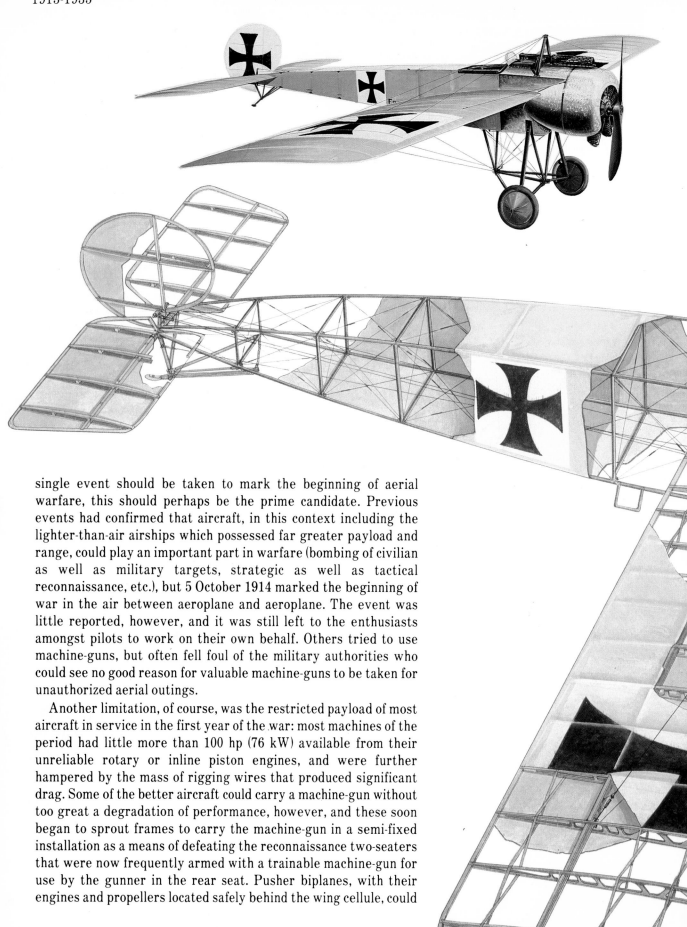

single event should be taken to mark the beginning of aerial warfare, this should perhaps be the prime candidate. Previous events had confirmed that aircraft, in this context including the lighter-than-air airships which possessed far greater payload and range, could play an important part in warfare (bombing of civilian as well as military targets, strategic as well as tactical reconnaissance, etc.), but 5 October 1914 marked the beginning of war in the air between aeroplane and aeroplane. The event was little reported, however, and it was still left to the enthusiasts amongst pilots to work on their own behalf. Others tried to use machine-guns, but often fell foul of the military authorities who could see no good reason for valuable machine-guns to be taken for unauthorized aerial outings.

Another limitation, of course, was the restricted payload of most aircraft in service in the first year of the war: most machines of the period had little more than 100 hp (76 kW) available from their unreliable rotary or inline piston engines, and were further hampered by the mass of rigging wires that produced significant drag. Some of the better aircraft could carry a machine-gun without too great a degradation of performance, however, and these soon began to sprout frames to carry the machine-gun in a semi-fixed installation as a means of defeating the reconnaissance two-seaters that were now frequently armed with a trainable machine-gun for use by the gunner in the rear seat. Pusher biplanes, with their engines and propellers located safely behind the wing cellule, could

Below left: The Germans' answer to the Morane-Saulnier Type L was the Fokker E I, essentially the M.5k monoplane fitted with a fixed machine-gun with synchroniser gear. The result was the first expression of genuine fighter armament, though the combination of an extremely flimsy airframe and 80-hp (60-kW) Oberursel U-0 rotary was at best mediocre. Despite its failings, the E I was the first true fighter, and gave the Germans a tactical edge explored to the full by their most aggressive pilots.

Far left and below: The E III was an improved version of the E II, itself an up-engined version of the E I. The E III was the Germans' main fighter in the first part of 1916, and was capable of 87 mph (140 km/h). Early examples had the Parabellum machine-gun, changed in later models for the MG 08/15, generally called the Spandau after its place of manufacture.

easily be fitted with a fixed or trainable machine-gun firing forwards, but the pusher biplanes generally available for front-line service at the time lacked the performance to make them effective in the aerial warfare role. The most impressive machine-gun of the period was the Vickers gas-operated gun evolved from the original Maxim gun, which had also spawned equivalents to the Vickers such as the German MG08: Vickers was also involved in the design and manufacture of aircraft, and had foreseen the need for armed aircraft with the performance to catch and outmanoeuvre enemy aircraft. Even before World War I, therefore, the company had produced an effective pusher type, the Vickers FB (fighting biplane), with provision for a forward-firing machine-gun, but this and other attempts along the same lines had foundered for lack of comparable pre-war forethought by the authorities, who saw the need only for cheaper two-seaters used in the scouting rather than fighting role.

Tractor aircraft, on the other hand, offered considerably higher performance and had their propellers in the nose. This meant that while the pilots had the performance to catch and engage their targets, they had to rig their machine-guns to fire outward at an angle of 30° or more so that the bullets would miss the propeller disc. This allowed the creation of a useful volume of fire, but did nothing to overcome the acute problems of aiming an offset weapon.

Below: The Bristol Scout was an impressive British biplane dating from 1913, and possessing admirable performance on its 110-hp (82-kW) Clerget rotary. It was also strong and agile, and with effective armament it could have been an effective fighter in 1914-15. As it was, pilots had to use rifles or extemporised mountings for Lewis guns.

What was needed was a simple yet reliable system of interrupting the fire of the machine-gun installed in a high-performance tractor aeroplane: fitted between the propeller disc and the machine-gun, this would allow the fire of the gun to be halted when a propeller blade was in the line of fire, and so make feasible the installation of a machine-gun firing along the aeroplane's line of flight and, just as importantly, along the pilot's natural line of vision, so easing the problem of aiming and firing accurately. This was a problem that had been addressed before World War I by a number of pioneers, most notably the Russian pilot Poplavko, the Swiss inventor Franz Schneider and the French designer Raymond Saulnier. All three had completed and tested primitive devices, but though these had worked modestly well within the limitations of their design, all three failed to a certain extent because of the unreliability of the ammunition's performance, which made it impossible to synchronise the devices accurately.

In an effort to save expensive propellers from destruction, Saulnier had fitted each blade of the propeller of his test aeroplane with a wedge-shaped steel deflector designed to ward off any bullet that would otherwise strike the blade, and this formed the origin of the first true 'fighter system'. Saulnier was still working on his system in 1915 when he was visited by Roland Garros, a pre-war test pilot and currently serving with the French air arm. Garros already knew of Saulnier's work, and now persuaded the aircraft designer to let him use the Morane-Saulnier Type L parasol-wing monoplane with the deflector plates but without the troublesome interrupter gear.

This aeroplane type was in service as a scout, and its performance

Above: **The Sopwith Pup was a great fighter, making up in tractability and precise handling for its lack of outright performance and single machine-gun.**

Above: The Spad S.7 was a real fighter's fighter, with first-rate performance and strength matched to adequate firepower and agility. Many French and Italian aces flew the S.7 to notable effect.

had already persuaded the French authorities to permit its employment with a number of extemporised armament mountings, including a light machine-gun located above the wing centre section to fire forward over the propeller disc. Such an expedient has been adopted on a number of aircraft operated by several countries, and may be regarded as an interim step towards the creation of a true fighter: it allowed the gun to be fired directly ahead, but was not very easy to aim and was decidedly difficult to reload. The standard light machine-gun in ground and aerial use by the Allies at the time was the 0.303-in (7.7-mm) Lewis gun, designed by an American and built under licence in Belgium and the U.K. The weapon did not require its bulky forced-draught cooling system in the aerial role, but needed fairly frequent changes of ammunition drum. This was located over the gun's receiver, and held either 47 or in later form 97 rounds. The gun was sometimes located on a quadrant mounting so that the pilot could pull the weapon back towards the cockpit when the magazine needed changing, but as often as not the pilot had to stand, fumble off the spent magazine and fit a fresh magazine, which was of course weighty and prone to being caught by the slipstream. The German equivalent to the Lewis was the 7.9-mm (0.31-in) Parabellum, but as this was fed by means of a flexible canvas belt an over-wing mounting was not practical, and it was used mainly as a defensive gun in two-seater aircraft.

In March 1915 Garros took his deflector-fitted Type L to the front, and on 1 April 1915 a new era in warfare was opened when this intrepid French pilot closed in to within 100-ft (30-m) of an unsuspecting German aeroplane, which saw no threat in the French single-seater, and downed it with an accurately placed burst of fire. The time of the fighter had dawned. Garros went from strength to strength, and in the following days shot down another three German aircraft. But the lashed-up armament system that made Garros very

Right: The Airco D.H.2 was the equipment of the first dedicated fighter squadron in British service, and as such was a capable though unexceptional aeroplane. The type was delivered with a nose-mounted gun that could be moved in elevation, but pilots soon found greater capability with the gun fixed and the whole aeroplane pointed at the target.

Below and bottom: Numerically the most important German fighter of 1917-18, the Albatros D V was a modest development of the D III but was generally outmatched in performance and strength by the newer Allied fighters.

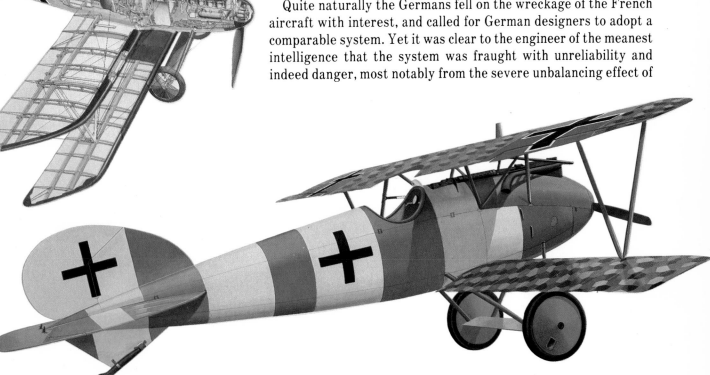

nearly the world's first ace was also his undoing: during another engagement his sorely-tried rotary engine failed and Garros came down behind the German lines. This was a feature of Allied air operations throughout the war, for the prevailing westerly wind tended to carry aircraft with engine failure across the lines into German territory (or indeed to keep aircraft operating behind the German front on that side of the line), whereas German aircraft generally operated close over the lines, and were thus carried back towards safety in the event of engine failure.

Quite naturally the Germans fell on the wreckage of the French aircraft with interest, and called for German designers to adopt a comparable system. Yet it was clear to the engineer of the meanest intelligence that the system was fraught with unreliability and indeed danger, most notably from the severe unbalancing effect of

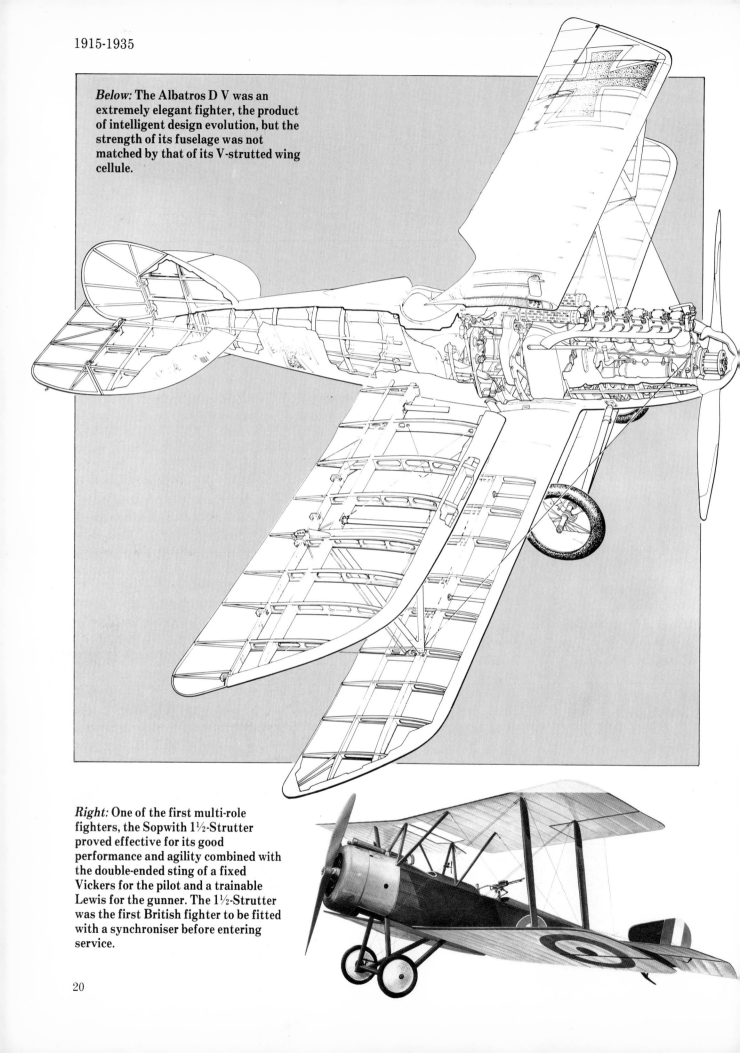

Below: The Albatros D V was an extremely elegant fighter, the product of intelligent design evolution, but the strength of its fuselage was not matched by that of its V-strutted wing cellule.

Right: One of the first multi-role fighters, the Sopwith 1½-Strutter proved effective for its good performance and agility combined with the double-ended sting of a fixed Vickers for the pilot and a trainable Lewis for the gunner. The 1½-Strutter was the first British fighter to be fitted with a synchroniser before entering service.

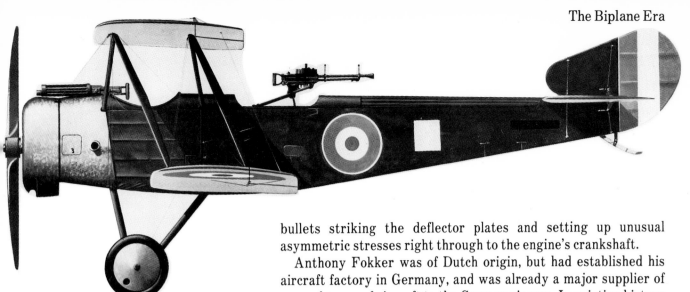

bullets striking the deflector plates and setting up unusual asymmetric stresses right through to the engine's crankshaft.

Anthony Fokker was of Dutch origin, but had established his aircraft factory in Germany, and was already a major supplier of several types of aircraft to the German air arm. In aviation history Fokker remains a controversial figure whose real nature and capabilities are disguised by his self-adulatory claims, but there is little doubt that Fokker was engineer enough to see that a system better than the Saulnier deflector plates could be produced without difficulty. Fokker later claimed that the interrupter gear was his own creation, but the evidence points to a pair of the company's engineers. Within two days of the capture of Garros and his machine, these men had produced the world's first genuinely practical interrupter gear. This should more properly be called a synchroniser gear for, once the trigger had been pressed by the pilot, such an engine-driven system fires the gun when the propeller blades are safely out of the line of fire whereas, as its name indicates, the interrupter gear halts the fire of the gun when a blade is in the line of fire.

The importance of the synchroniser was immediately apparent, and the type was ordered into production on a development of the Fokker M5k monoplane used to evaluate the prototype system. Thus was born the Fokker E I *Eindecker* (monoplane), the world's first genuinely effective fighter. A first victory for the type was claimed by Kurt Wintgens on 15 July 1915, but this was unconfirmed as the victim came down on the Allied side of the lines.

Below: **Though known universally as the Sopwith 1½-Strutter, this attractive biplane was designated Type 9700 by its originating service, the Royal Navy, and as the Sopwith Two-Seater by the Royal Flying Corps.**

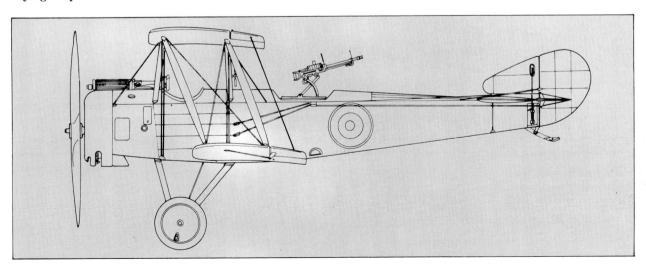

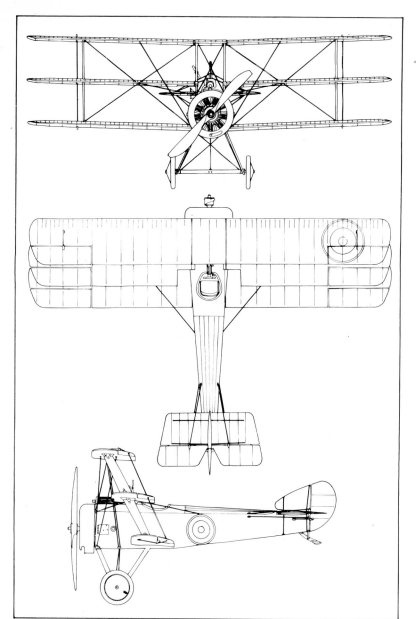

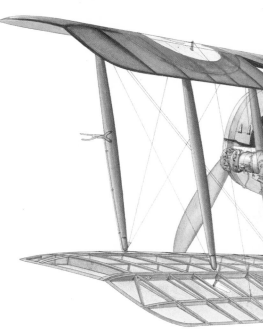

Left: **Key to the Sopwith Triplane's success was the combination of the basic Sopwith fuselage and empennage with the cellule of compact but large-area triplane wing.**

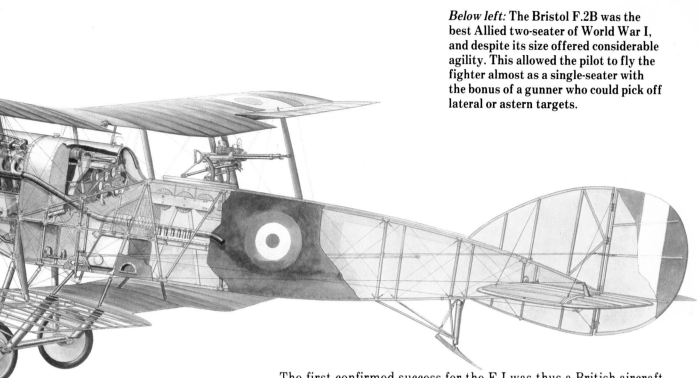

The first confirmed success for the E I was thus a British aircraft that fell to Max Immelmann on 1 August. Production of the E I was limited, for the type was powered by an Oberursel U-0 rotary engine whose 80 hp (60 kW) provided only indifferent performance. In September the improved E II began to reach the front, with 100-hp (76-kW) available from its U-I engine, and this soon began to make a significant impact on Allied air operations. The *Eindecker* can in no way be considered an effective fighter (or indeed a good aeroplane by any objective criteria), but its possession of the world's first effective air-to-air armament system turned it into a potentially decisive aircraft, especially in the hands of aggressive pilots schooled in the tactics evolved by Immelmann and his mentor, the great Oswald Boelcke. The most important tactic attributable to Immelmann was a dive out of the sun towards an unsuspecting target, a quick burst of fire and a continued dive towards safety, followed by an 'Immelmann turn' (a zoom climb with a half-roll from the top of the resultant loop) to regain height and the tactical advantage before another dive attack from the opposite direction if required. But Immelmann was essentially a loner who could not readily impart his ideas to others. Moreover, Immelmann was killed after scoring 15 rapid victories.

Far more important, therefore, was Boelcke, who must be regarded as the true father of fighter combat. Boelcke was a professional soldier with a keen analytical mind as well as inherent skills. He was able to analyse how his own victories were scored and how the likelihood of such victories could be increased, and also to pass on the lessons of his success and tactical thinking. Although he sometimes used the Immelmann type of attack, Boelcke favoured the stalking attack, in which he tracked an unsuspecting two-seater from below and behind, in the gunner's blind spot, before closing in

Left: Mount of many aces, the Nieuport 17 was evolved from the Nieuport 11 with a slightly larger and considerably stronger airframe to make full use of a more powerful engine and a synchronised machine-gun.

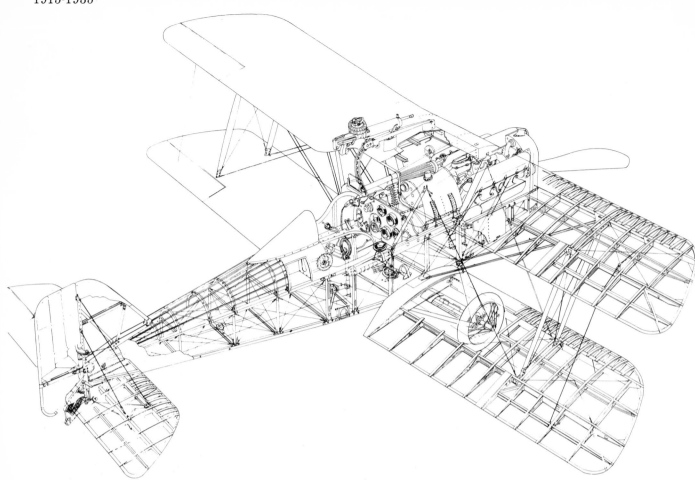

to decisively short range so that all the bullets would strike home when he pulled up the nose of his fighter and fired a short burst: this reduced the problem of deflection shooting (required to build in a lead component against an enemy manoeuvring in one or more planes), and economised on ammunition expenditure, thereby increasing the chances of engaging another target successfully.

The *Eindecker* fighters were initially allocated in penny packets to existing two-seater units for use in the escort role, but it was one of Boelcke's greatest successes that he appreciated the importance of dedicated fighter units that would not be tied to the two-seaters but operate independently to tackle the enemy's aircraft. Thus the first single-seat fighter units began to emerge, and within this new organisational structure Boelcke and his men began to take an increasing toll of Allied aircraft using the new tactics. The German effort was boosted by the arrival of the E III version of the *Eindecker* with a number of improvements and generally with one or two examples of the 7.9-mm MG08/15 machine-gun (a lightened version of Germany's standard ground-based machine-gun for the sustained-fire role, and a notably reliable weapon) in place of the original Parabellum of the same calibre. The ultimate expression of the series was the E IV, of which only a few were built with the troublesome two-row Oberursel rotary engine.

The *Eindecker* was the fighter type largely responsible for what

Above: A product of the Royal Aircraft Factory, the S.E.5a was strong and powerful, allowing steep diving attacks or escapes without fear of structural failure. The type was also notable for its stability as a gun platform, and this was a factor that endeared it to many British aces.

has become known to history as the 'Fokker Scourge' that began in October 1916. Though it was little appreciated at the time, the period witnessed a marked increase in the proportion of overall losses attributable to operational rather than non-operational reasons. The German single-seat units grew in strength and capability until the early months of 1916, when they were redesignated as *Kampfeinsitzerkommando* units, while the Allies had nothing with which to tackle the menace directly. However, the poor flight performance of the *Eindecker* became a real liability when faced with a solid defence of several aircraft (normally of three-aircraft Vs), and the French led the way with formations whose gunners could provide mutual defence. Thus the losses were reduced, and the Allies started a major effort to produce a counter to the *Eindecker*.

The Allied response is epitomised by one French and one British aircraft: the French contender was the excellent little Nieuport 11 Bébé, and the British offering the Airco D.H.2. The Bébé entered service in the same month as the E III, and for lack of an Allied synchroniser gear was fitted with an overwing Lewis gun: despite the fact that it had only the same power as the E I it had performance genuinely superior to that of the E III, and was in addition highly manoeuvrable with delightful handling characteristics. The British were also hampered by lack of a synchroniser gear, but instead opted for a trim pusher layout with a trainable (subsequently fixed) Lewis gun in the nose. The D.H.2 began to enter service in February 1916, and again offered greater performance and agility than the *Eindecker*. Production of both

Below: An unusual feature of the RAF S.E.5a was the armament installation of one synchronised Vickers in the fuselage and one unsynchronised Lewis above the centre section of the upper wing. Most contemporary fighters used a neater installation of two synchronised guns.

The S.E.5a was at home at all altitudes, its steadiness making it effective at low level and its high rate of climb coming to the fore at medium and high altitudes.

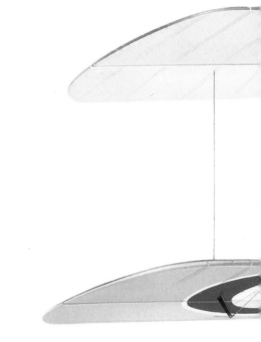

Allied fighters was slow, but by the beginning of March it was discernible that the tide was turning against the *Eindecker*. This trend soon became almost a flood, and by the summer of 1916 the Bébé had completely mastered the *Eindecker* over the Battle of Verdun, while the D.H.2, supported by the lumbering but prickly RFC F.E.2b two-seat pusher, had secured mastery over the Germans above the battlefields of the Somme.

Further capability became available as the first Allied fighters with synchroniser gear began to reach the front in the early spring of 1916. The first of these was the superlative Sopwith 1½-Strutter, the world's first multi-role combat aircraft with capability as a fighter, reconnaissance aircraft and bomber. Despite its two-seat configuration the 1½-Strutter was a good performer on its 110-hp (82-kW) Clerget rotary, and displayed beautiful handling characteristics. But the most important single aspect of the 1½-Strutter was its armament, comprising a synchronised forward-firing Vickers for the pilot and a trainable Lewis on a Scarff ring mounting for the gunner. Crews were quick to appreciate the combat advantages of a tractable yet manoeuvrable platform with both fixed and trainable guns, and the type rapidly became a mainstay of the British army and navy air arms, as well as being supplied to the French, who also built larger numbers of the type under licence.

Next into service was the classic Nieuport 17 single-seat fighter, successor to the Bébé with a larger and stronger airframe mated to a 110-hp Le Rhône or 130-hp (97-kW) Clerget rotary for sprightly performance. The Nieuport 17 could be armed with a synchronised Vickers and an over-wing Lewis, but was generally flown with only the former so that the service ceiling, rate of climb and manoeuvrability would not be compromised. The Nieuport 17 occupies an important niche in aviation history, for while the E-

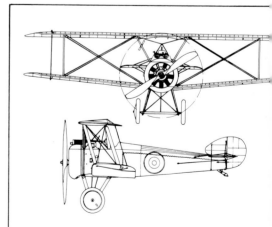

Above: All views of the Camel, otherwise the 'vicious little beast', emphasise the concentration of mass in the forward fuselage around the centre of gravity.

Below and below right: **The Sopwith Camel, officially designated the Sopwith Biplane F.1, was the most successful fighter of World War I, offering its pilots a highly effective yet unquantifiable blend of performance, agility and firepower.**

series may be regarded as the first fighters, the Nieuport 17 should be considered the world's first truly effective single-seat fighter: before this sturdy machine no other single-seater had combined performance, agility and firepower, the three basic characteristics by which all subsequent fighters have been judged. The British paid the same compliment to the Nieuport 17 as the French had conferred on the 1½-Strutter, accepting substantial numbers for service with the Royal Flying Corps but not going so far as to manufacture it.

The summer of 1916 was thus a happy time for the Allies, while the Germans began to suffer the consequences of failing to

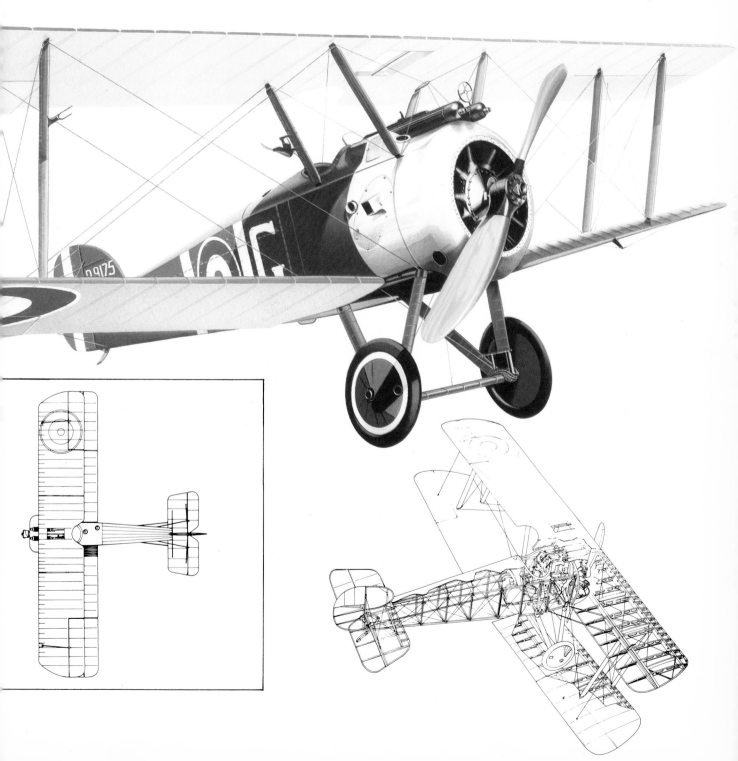

supersede the *Eindecker* and other first-generation fighters such as the Fokker D I and D II and the Halberstadt D II biplanes. Yet the Germans retained an organisational superiority, the extemporised *Kampfeinsitzerkommando* units being replaced in the late summer of 1916 by the first properly constituted fighter squadrons, the *Jagdstaffeln* soon grouped into *Jagdgeschwader* fighter wings under capable leaders. The best of the fighter squadrons was Boelcke's Jasta 2, whose capabilities are exemplified by 76 'kills' for seven losses in the period from September to November 1916. To match this revised organisational pattern, the Germans now introduced an effective single-seat fighter in the form of the Albatros D I and D II, which entered combat in early September and October 1916 respectively. Using virtually identical airframes and powered by the 150-hp (112-kW) Benz Bz-III and 160-hp (119-kW)

Left: **Marking the start of a new design concept for its manufacturer, the Nieuport 28 was not in itself very successful, but paved the way for the post-war Nieuport 29, which was an excellent fighter.**

Mercedes D-III inline engines respectively, the Albatros D I and D II were the chief mounts of the *Jastas* until supplemented but never entirely replaced by later fighters from the spring of 1917. Both the D I and D II possessed adequate performance, but their real strength lay in their armament, the Germans having moved one step up the weapon ladder to introduce a fixed forward-firing armament of two MG08/15 machine-guns. Such an installation, with the breeches located within reach of the pilot so that he could clear the jams to which all machine-guns of the period were prone, lasted until the mid-1930s. And to this extent the early Albatros fighters must be considered definitive.

These two fighters were also immensely strong, largely from the use of a plywood-covered fuselage. The D I suffered from the fact that the upper wing was slightly above the pilot's line of sight, thereby masking his view forward and upward, so on the D II the upper wing was lowered slightly to rest on a centre section cabane of splayed N-struts rather than a trestle arrangement.

The only two Allied fighters with a chance of matching the Albatros D I and D II were the Spad S.7 and Sopwith Pup, which both entered service in September 1916. The S.7 was a French design of immense strength and high performance, but with only a single Vickers was outgunned by the German fighters. The S.7 was flown by many of France's aces, who appreciated the type's strength and stability as a gun platform, and was also flown by the Belgians, British and Italians amongst others. The Pup, so named for its resemblance to the larger 1½-Strutter, was phenomenally underpowered with only an 80-hp Le Rhône rotary, but was exceptionally lightly loaded and thus secured adequate performance but completely unrivalled levels of agility. It could thus live with the new Germans' fighters, but suffered the same disadvantage as the S.7 in having only a single gun. The agility displayed by the Pup was further extended in Sopwith's next offering, the Triplane that began to enter service in November 1916. This was essentially an up-engined version of the Pup with triplane wings to offer the very useful advantages of improved pilot view, greater area, and reduced chord: the result was excellent agility and a superb rate of climb. But again the armament was just a single gun, and despite the performance advantages of these three Allied fighters the Germans retained and even expanded their tactical superiority in the spring of 1917, which culminated in the so-called 'Bloody April' when the Royal Flying Corps and, to a lesser extent, the French air force suffered catastrophic losses, especially to the two-seater squadrons operating wholly obsolete tactical reconnaissance and artillery-spotting aircraft such as the RFC B.E.2 series.

The reason lies not with the aircraft but with organisation and pilots. The Allies had larger numbers of fighters with superior flight performance, but were taking the air war to the Germans with generally inexperienced pilots. The Germans, on the other hand, had adequate fighters flown by highly experienced pilots such as Manfred von Richthofen, who were content to engage the Allied forces only when the German fighter squadrons could secure the tactical advantage. The Albatros D I and D II were still adequate,

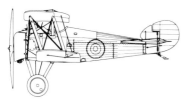

Above: Front and side elevations of the Sopwith Snipe confirm the type's derivation from the Camel.

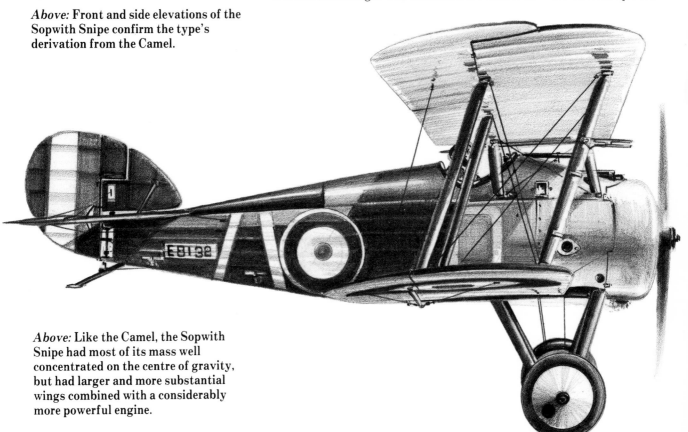

Above: Like the Camel, the Sopwith Snipe had most of its mass well concentrated on the centre of gravity, but had larger and more substantial wings combined with a considerably more powerful engine.

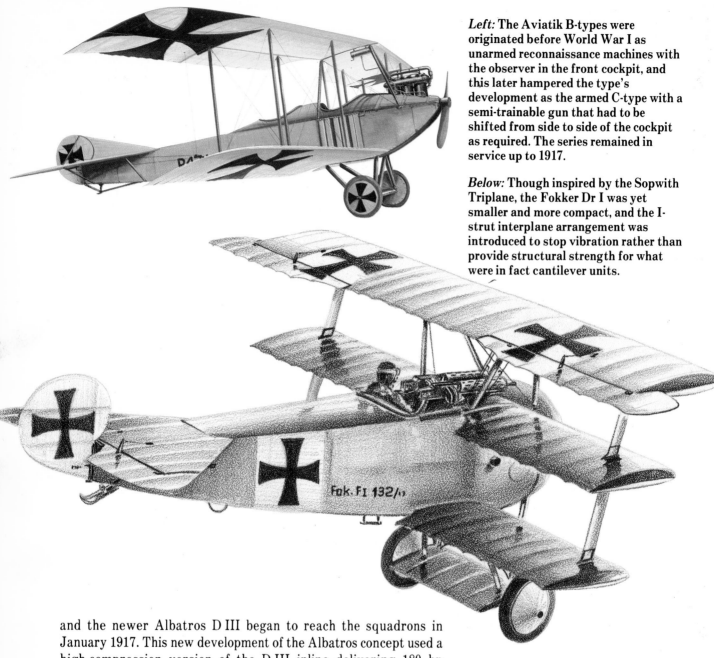

Left: The Aviatik B-types were originated before World War I as unarmed reconnaissance machines with the observer in the front cockpit, and this later hampered the type's development as the armed C-type with a semi-trainable gun that had to be shifted from side to side of the cockpit as required. The series remained in service up to 1917.

Below: Though inspired by the Sopwith Triplane, the Fokker Dr I was yet smaller and more compact, and the I-strut interplane arrangement was introduced to stop vibration rather than provide structural strength for what were in fact cantilever units.

and the newer Albatros D III began to reach the squadrons in January 1917. This new development of the Albatros concept used a high-compression version of the D-III inline delivering 180 hp (134 kW), and had better performance than the D II. Tactically the fighter was improved by the use of a narrow-chord lower wing (braced to the upper wing by V-format interplane struts), which had been inspired by that of the Nieuport 17 to give the pilot enhanced downward fields of vision, but this advantage was offset by the new wing cellule's inherent structural weakness: the lower wing tended to twist and break away in a high-speed dive.

The situation was about to be redressed in favour of the Allies, however, as a new generation of fighters began to reach the squadrons in the see-saw technical battle characteristic of modern war. First into the fray was the Bristol F.2 Fighter, later dubbed the 'Brisfit' and one of the most successful and longest-lived aircraft to serve with the British air force before the jet age. The F.2 was fast

and moderately agile, and followed in the steps of the 1½-Strutter in being a two-seat fighter, though in this instance with a single fixed and one or two trainable guns. The initial model was the F.2A with the 190-hp (142-kW) Rolls-Royce Falcon, and this suffered a disastrous service debut when four out of six F.2As fell to von Richthofen's Jasta 11 early in April 1917. The crews had treated their aircraft like conventional two-seaters, flying a formation designed to optimise the gunners' chances. It was soon realised that the new Bristol aeroplane could and should be handled like a single-seater, with the gunner's weapon(s) available as 'bonus'. Once this concept had been digested the Bristol Fighter went from strength to strength, especially after the arrival later in April of the first F.2Bs with improved pilot visibility and other improvements. The F.2B was steadily upgraded, and ended the war with the 275-hp (205-kW) Falcon III and performance superior to that of many single-seat fighters. So capable did the F.2B prove in service that enormous orders were placed, and when production of the airframe began to outstrip that of engines, a number of alternative powerplants were tried, though none of these proved as good as the Falcon. The U.S. Army also ordered the type in mass production in the U.S.A., but

Above: Though too late for widespread service in World War I, and possessing an anachronistic appearance with its parasol wing and 110-hp (82-kW) Oberursel U-II rotary, the Fokker D VIII was potentially a decisive fighter with twin-gun armament but, more importantly, phenomenal agility and highly impressive climb and dive characteristics.

Below: The Fokker D VII was possibly the finest fighter to see extensive service in World War I, much of its success stemming from the steel-tube fuselage and plywood-covered wings, which conferred magnificent strength.

Above: The FB was the first flying-boat produced by Hansa-Brandenburg (in 1915) but used mainly by Austria-Hungary. The type was produced as an observation type, but the good position of its trainable machine-gun made it at times an effective escort.

this massive programme was spoiled by the U.S. aero industry's lack of experience with mass production of aircraft, and by the decision to use the powerful 400-hp (298-kW) Liberty 12 engine, which made the aeroplane nose heavy. The Bristol Fighter's combat capability is attested by the fact that seven pilots scored between 20 and 30 'kills' while flying the type, and many gunners in the type also built up enviable success figures.

The two other British fighters that checked and finally broke German superiority in the first half of 1917 were the Royal Aircraft Factory S.E.5 and the Sopwith Camel. These complemented each other in service: the S.E.5 was a superb gun platform, possessed great structural strength, and had admirable performance most impressive in the figures for speed and ceiling; the Camel, on the other hand, had adequate performance but quite exceptional agility. The S.E.5 series began to enter service in April 1917 in its initial S.E.5 form with a 150-hp (112-kW) Hispano-Suiza engine, but was rapidly succeeded by the up-engined S.E.5a with the 200-hp (149-kW) Hispano-Suiza. This latter proved somewhat unreliable, and most S.E.5a fighters were produced with the Wolseley Viper, which was based on the Hispano-Suiza engine but offered greater reliability and the same power. Oddly enough, the armament of the S.E.5 series was fitted with a hybrid armament system still inferior to that of the twin-gun German fighters: the type did in fact have two guns, but these comprised a single fixed Vickers in the forward fuselage and operating in conjunction with a Constantinesco synchroniser, and a Lewis carried on a quadrant mounting over the wing to fire clear over the propeller disc without the need for a synchroniser. The upper gun was fired by means of a Bowden cable, and had to be pulled back and down towards the cockpit for the pilot to change the ammunition drum. One tactical advantage did result from the use of such a mounting, however: pilots could close up under the target's blind spot, and then pull back the Lewis to rake the underside of the fuselage without the need to pull up the nose of their own aircraft and thus lose speed. The S.E.5 was flown by many of Britain's greatest aces, and the three who stand out above all others on the type are Edward Mannock (73 victories), William Bishop (72 victories) and William McCudden (57 victories).

The Camel was derived directly from the concept of the Pup, but was more compact, better armed, and in its definitive form fitted with the powerful 130-hp Clerget or 150-hp Bentley B.R.1 engine. Some examples were also produced with the 100-hp Gnome Monosoupape and 100-hp Le Rhône rotaries. The armament was the first British use of twin fixed Vickers guns, in this instance operated in conjunction with a variety of synchronisers: the guns were located in the standard position in the upper half of the forward fuselage, the breeches being enclosed in a hump of the upper decking, and it was this last feature that gave the fighter the name by which it is universally known in preference to the official

Below: The Macchi M.7 was evolved from the M.5 in 1918 as a flying-boat fighter to cope with types such as the Hansa-Brandenburg FB.

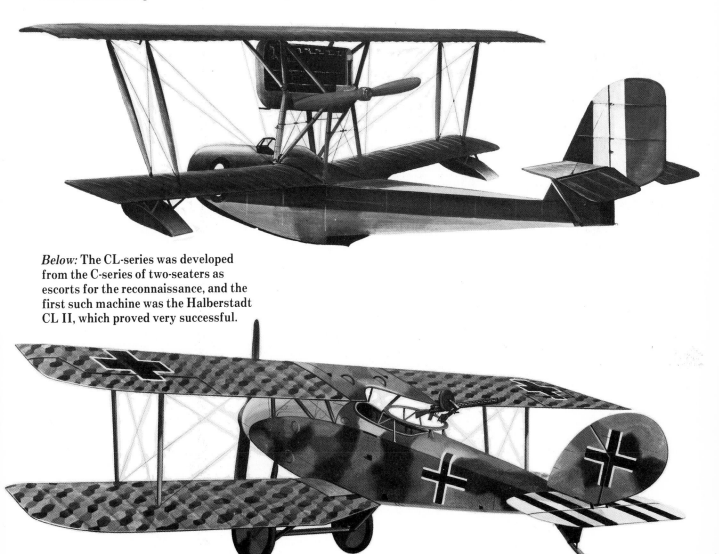

Below: The CL-series was developed from the C-series of two-seaters as escorts for the reconnaissance, and the first such machine was the Halberstadt CL II, which proved very successful.

designation Sopwith F.1 (or 2F.1 for the naval version with shorter-span wings and an armament of one Vickers and one over-wing Lewis guns). An indication of the Camel's exceptionally compact design is provided by the fact that the fighter's main mass (propeller, engine, guns, ammunition, fuel, and pilot) was contained in the forward 7 ft (2.13 m) of the fuselage, and this concentration is one of the two factors that contributed to the Camel's exceptional agility by reducing heavy moments. The other factor was the torque of the rotary engine, which allowed phenomenally rapid turns to the right: if taken at a disadvantage, the Camel pilot could break right and almost invariably arrive in the tactical advantageous position on his opponent's tail. Yet this agility was not without its disadvantages too: a concomitant of the superb right-hand turning performance was a tendency for the nose to drop, and unless corrected rapidly by rudder movement this developed swiftly into a spin that caused the deaths of an unfortunately high number of less experienced pilots who fell foul of this trait when they had insufficient height (and in some cases skill) to get out of the spin. The Clerget rotary was also a tricky powerplant to operate, and unless its mixture was weakened after take-off it tended to choke, causing the aircraft to stall at a height from which it was impossible to recover.

Yet the capabilities of the Camel outweighed its trickiness by a considerable margin, and the Camel was built to a total of 5,490 examples compared with 5,205 examples of the S.E.5 series. The Camel also possesses the distinction of being the most successful fighter of World War I, the type being credited with the destruction of no fewer than 1,294 aircraft in aerial combat. Like the S.E.5 the Camel too had its particular advocates and exponents, the highest-scoring of these being Raymond Collishaw (63 victories). And forever linked with the Camel must be the death of von Richthofen on 21 April 1918: some still claim that the legendary 'Red Baron', who had scored 80 victories to make him the premier ace of World

Above: **The Thomas-Morse S-4C was produced as a lightweight fighter for the U.S. Army, but by 1917 was completely outclassed by European fighters and thus used as an advanced trainer, with an 80-hp (60-kW) Le Rhône rotary in place of the 100-hp (76-kW) Gnome originally proposed for the fighter.**

The Halberstadt CL IV was a capable two-seat escort fighter developed from the CL II. With a 160-hp (119-kW) Mercedes D-III inline, the type attained only a modest 103 mph (165 km/h), but was well armed even by the standards of 1918 with two fixed MG 08/15 guns and one trainable Parabellum gun.

War I, was brought down by the ground fire of an Australian machine-gunner, but it remains more likely that he was killed by a Canadian pilot, Captain A.R. Brown, who was flying a Camel.

These British fighters were paralleled in French service by two useful fighters, the Nieuport 24 and the Spad S.13 (sometimes rendered S.XIII in the same way as the S.7 is frequently presented as the S.VII). The Nieuport 24 was derived from the Nieuport 17 and began to enter service in the spring of 1917. The type bore marked similarities to its predecessor, but introduced a well-streamlined fuselage of rounded section and also the 130-hp Le Rhône rotary in place of the Nieuport 17's 110-hp engine from the same manufacturer. The result was usefully increased performance, especially in speed and rate of climb, though the armament remained a single machine-gun. On French aircraft this was usually a synchronised Vickers, while examples flown by the British generally sported an over-wing Lewis. The ultimate expression of this basic design concept was the Nieuport 27, in essence a refined Nieuport 24 with rounded tips to its horizontal flying surfaces, plus a more curved vertical tail. The philosophy that had seen development from the Nieuport 11 to Nieuport 27 was now played out, for the basic structure was incapable of accepting further power which, in any event, would have overtaxed the almost sesquiplane arrangement of broad-chord upper wing connected to a narrow-chord lower wing by interplane V-struts.

The S.13 was a more advanced aeroplane, derived closely from the S.7 but enlarged and fitted with the considerably more powerful 200-hp Hispano-Suiza inline, and later a 220-hp (164-kW) version of the same engine. These engines provided better performance despite the greater weight of the airframe and the upgraded

35

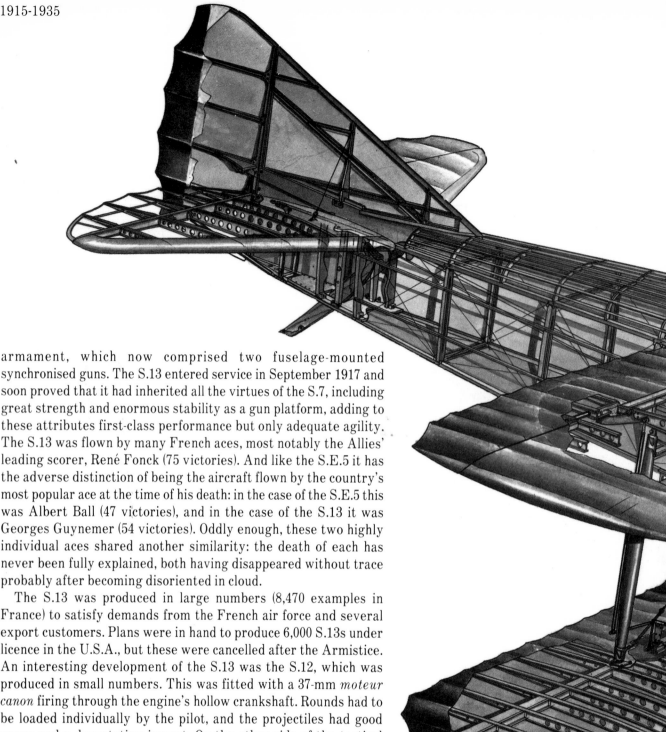

armament, which now comprised two fuselage-mounted synchronised guns. The S.13 entered service in September 1917 and soon proved that it had inherited all the virtues of the S.7, including great strength and enormous stability as a gun platform, adding to these attributes first-class performance but only adequate agility. The S.13 was flown by many French aces, most notably the Allies' leading scorer, René Fonck (75 victories). And like the S.E.5 it has the adverse distinction of being the aircraft flown by the country's most popular ace at the time of his death: in the case of the S.E.5 this was Albert Ball (47 victories), and in the case of the S.13 it was Georges Guynemer (54 victories). Oddly enough, these two highly individual aces shared another similarity: the death of each has never been fully explained, both having disappeared without trace probably after becoming disoriented in cloud.

The S.13 was produced in large numbers (8,470 examples in France) to satisfy demands from the French air force and several export customers. Plans were in hand to produce 6,000 S.13s under licence in the U.S.A., but these were cancelled after the Armistice. An interesting development of the S.13 was the S.12, which was produced in small numbers. This was fitted with a 37-mm *moteur canon* firing through the engine's hollow crankshaft. Rounds had to be loaded individually by the pilot, and the projectiles had good range and a devastating impact. On the other side of the tactical coin, however, the cannon produced a large cloud of smoke whenever it was fired, and the niceties of loading proved too much for most pilots. The final wartime expression of the Spad design philosophy was the S.17, which was a larger and yet stronger version of the S.13 fitted with a 300-hp (224-kW) Hispano-Suiza engine. This model was introduced in the summer of 1918, and only a few were built.

The comparative ease with which fighters could be designed, evaluated and placed into production during World War I meant that though the types described above were the main Allied fighters

Above: The family resemblance of the
Spad S.13 to the earlier S.7 is plain to
see. Compared with its predecessor the
S.13 offered greater power and heavier
firepower, but also introduced
aerodynamic modifications to enhance
control sensitivity and manoeuvrability.

of 1917 and 1918, they were supplemented by several other models. With hindsight the historian can only quibble with the division of effort that this caused, whereas the enthusiast can only be grateful for the wealth of interesting types that was thus made possible. It is also worth pointing out that while the production and support of several in-service types had their problems and adverse effects, such a practice also allowed the employment of engines that might otherwise not have found an application. Central control of development was not a feature of the time, so a multiplication of effort was inevitable. In these circumstances the building of several types was perhaps the best way to make effective use of surplus engines and the like.

On the British side these lesser types included the Airco D.H.5, the Bristol M.1C, the Sopwith 5F.1 Dolphin and the Sopwith 7F.1 Snipe. The D.H.5 was designed by Geoffrey de Havilland as successor to his D.H.2, and sought to combine the fields of vision possible with a pusher aeroplane with the performance of a tractor layout, in this instance using a 130-hp Le Rhône rotary. The main feature of the design was therefore a backward-staggered upper wing, which succeeded admirably in fulfilling the primary design aim. The D.H.5 entered service late in 1916, but enjoyed only a short frontline career in its intended fighter role. The type proved to have inadequate performance at heights above 10,000 ft (3,050 m), and lost height rapidly during combat. Thereafter the D.H.5 enjoyed a successful secondary career as a ground-attack fighter, a role in which the wing layout and position of the single Vickers machine-gun proved most useful. Such a task also fell increasingly to other fighters, and not just those that had been superannuated as first-line combat fighters. So-called contact patrols had become increasingly important in 1916, allowing the high command to be apprised of their troops' forward positions by fighters sent out to support these direly pressed infantry at very low level with machine-gun fire and, increasingly, light bombs carried on racks under the fuselage.

The M.1C was an altogether more capable machine powered by a 110-hp Clerget rotary. Yet again the armament was a single Vickers, but the performance can only be regarded as excellent by the standards of the day. The reason for this is simple: the M.1C was a well-streamlined monoplane, and thus generated less drag than a comparable biplane. Handling was good, rate of climb excellent, and the pilot enjoyed large fields of vision. But the M.1C failed to find the official favour which it deserved, nominally for its comparatively high landing speed but in reality for the distrust entertained by the British authorities about the structural integrity of the monoplane. In fact the M.1C was a strong and agile aeroplane, but the 125 examples produced were relegated to operational life in secondary theatres, most notably Macedonia and Palestine.

Backward-staggered biplane wings were also a feature of the Dolphin, which began to enter service in January 1918. Powered by a 200-hp Hispano-Suiza inline, the Dolphin was designed as a high-altitude fighter and possessed an absolute ceiling of 21,000 ft

Below: **Introduced in 1932, the Boeing F4B-4 was a late expression of a basic design of great capability that had served the U.S. Army and U.S. Navy throughout the 1920s. This variant had a Townend ring round the Wasp B radial to reduce drag, and could touch 186 mph (299 km/h) at 6,000 ft (1,830m).**

Right: The Curtiss F6C-1 was the naval version of the U.S. Army's P-1, but intended for use by the U.S. Marine Corps as land-based fighters. They thus lacked carrier equipment, but could be used on twin-float alighting gear.

(6,400 m), but is of more interest as the first multi-gun fighter to enter operational service. The standard forward-firing armament of twin synchronised Vickers guns was retained, but in this application was supplemented by two Lewis guns on the open centre section of the upper wing, firing obliquely forward and upward. The upper wing was itself located fairly low over the fuselage, with the pilot's head protruding through it in a fashion dangerously vulnerable should the aeroplane turn over on landing. This did not endear the type to pilots, who also feared that in combat or a hard landing their heads would fly forward and hit the Lewis guns. The Lewis guns were usually removed for this reason, though one squadron relocated them to the lower wings outboard of the propeller disc to avoid any loss of firepower.

The Snipe was a development of the Camel with the 230-hp (172-kW) Bentley B.R.2 rotary. It retained many of the Camel's qualities and added a useful improvement in performance, and has been judged one of the best fighters in service at the time of the Armistice in November 1918, having begun to enter service in the last weeks before the war's end. The type went on to become the standard British fighter of the immediate post-war period, remaining in service until 1926. The type was also used in one of history's most epic dogfights. This occurred on 27 October 1918, when the Canadian ace Major William Barker was engaged by a force estimated at 60 German fighters. Barker was eventually forced down in the Allied lines with three wounds, but only after he had shot down four of his attackers and severely damaged several others. These were the last of Barker's 53 victories, and the pilot subsequently received the Victoria Cross for this feat.

The two most significant French fighters to enter only limited service were the Hanriot HD-1 and the Nieuport 28. The HD-1 can be considered the French equivalent to the Sopwith Pup, though it entered service somewhat later (in August 1917) and served mostly

Below: The Gloster Gorcock Mk I was an experimental fighter with the 525-hp (391-kW) Napier Lion VIII inline. Flown in 1925, it introduced mixed construction with a steel-framed fuselage and wooden wings.

Below: The Curtiss P-6 series was entensively used in the 1920s and 1930s by the U.S. Army, variants appearing with a bewildering variety of engines, cooling systems and, on occasion, superchargers, so paving the way for the introduction of more advanced monoplane fighters.

with the Belgian and Italian air forces. The type was powered by a 120-hp Le Rhône rotary and featured a single synchronised Vickers gun, and like the Pup was a delight to fly and also very sturdy. In a fashion similar to the S.13, the HD-1 was also developed with twin-float alighting gear for naval use. The Nieuport 28 marked the beginning of a new basic design concept for the company, with emphasis on an elegantly tapered fuselage and a conventional biplane wing configuration with parallel interplane struts. The type was powered by a 160-hp (119-kW) Gnome Monosoupape in deference to the company's continued adherence to this type of engine, and was thus comparatively underpowered when it entered service in early 1918. Performance was adequate, and a twin-gun synchronised armament was fitted, but as the French were already heavily committed to the S.13 the Nieuport 28 was used mainly by the fledgling American air force in France. The type's primary failing was a tendency to shed the fabric of its top wing in a steep dive, and this played a considerable part in inhibiting pilots from getting the best out of their mounts.

The Germans, meanwhile, had not been sitting idly by and letting the Allies secure the technological upper hand. This cannot disguise the fact that the Germans had placed too great a reliance on the Albatros D III, which in the event had achieved only a small performance advantage over the D II and had therefore been

Above: The Hawker Fury was a landmark in fighter design as the first such aircraft to reach speeds of more than 200 mph (322 km/h) in level flight. The lines were excellent, and the structure both strong and easily maintained.

Right: The Fury's predecessor was the Bristol Bulldog, which marked the apogee of the radial-engined British fighter derived directly from World War I experience.

outclassed by the newer Allied fighters very soon after its introduction. In the short term the upgraded Albatros D V was introduced with a high-compression Mercedes D-IIIa inline engine developing 180 hp, and with a wing cellule revised to a sesquiplane configuration clearly inspired by that of the Nieuport 17. A beautifully designed fuselage built of plywood provided good streamlining and an excellent structural base for the design, but this strength was unmatched by that of the wing cellule, which was fitted with interplane V-struts and proved disastrously prone to lower-wing twist and breakaway in steep dives. The type began to enter service in May 1917, and had to remain in production because there was nothing to replace it. Small improvement was effected in the D Va, which had a higher-compression engine for slightly more power, a completely oval-section fuselage with larger spinner for improved streamlining, and a rounded vertical tail. Both the D V and D Va soldiered on to the end of the war for lack of a replacement available in adequate numbers.

Great hopes were entertained for the Fokker Dr I and Pfalz D III, but in the event these hopes proved unfounded. Like several competing triplane designs, of which only this one type entered production, the Dr I was directly inspired by the Sopwith Triplane,

Right: Bulldogs became immensely popular with the public for their aerobatic capabilities, and also enjoyed very useful export sales to countries as diverse as Finland and Siam. With the former the type saw operational service in World War II.

Below: Though still carrying the standard fit of two 0.303-in (7.7-mm) Vickers guns, the Bulldog was a useful performer, being capable of 174 mph (280 km/h) on the 530 hp (395 kW) of its Bristol Jupiter supercharged radial.

and designed to provide Germany's pilots with a fighter possessing only modest performance but unrivalled rate of climb and turning performance. As the Germans were fighting defensively over their own lines, the former was judged essential to get the nimble little fighter rapidly to the height at which it could use its latter attribute to engage marauding Allied fighters. The concept was adequate if limited, and the Dr I appeared for service in August 1917 with a 110-hp Oberursel or Swedish-built Le Rhône rotary. The Dr I achieved some success in the hands of the aces, but was then withdrawn after a few disastrous crashes. The fault was found to lie with faulty workmanship, but when the type returned to service in December 1917 it was distrusted by its pilots and also wholly outclassed within even its limited operational role.

The Pfalz D III began to enter service in September 1917, and bore an overall similarity to the Albatros D III, including the same armament and powerplant. However, the fuselage was better streamlined and a superior biplane wing cellule was fitted, and the Germans hoped that performance might be increased to a useful degree. Yet again the hope proved vain, rate of climb and agility proving generally inferior to those of the Albatros D V. Both the Dr I and the Pfalz D III were thus allocated to the less experienced and less capable German fighter pilots, the aces preferring to use the Albatros D V and D Va until something better could be produced.

In January 1918 a competition was held for prototypes of a new standard fighter, all interested parties (including combat pilots) having the opportunity to fly and pass comment on the prototypes. The winner was the prototype of the fighter which entered service in May 1918 as the Fokker D VII, now generally considered to have been the best operational fighter of World War I. The specification called for the standard twin-gun armament and use of the 160/180-hp Mercedes D-III, though production D VIIs were offered with this engine or the 185-hp (138-kW) BMW IIIa, another of the first-class six-cylinder inline engines produced by Germany. Another interesting feature was the car-type nose radiator in place of the centre-section type that had been installed in the upper wing of most other German fighters with water-cooled engines. The centre-section location had permitted a fine nose entry for better performance, but meant that the pilot was showered with scalding water if the radiator was punctured: some designers had offset the radiator to one side, but a sideslip still resulted in a scalded pilot.

The D VII was designed by Reinhold Platz, who had also been responsible for the Dr I, and used the same combination of welded steel-tube fuselage and thick-section plywood-covered wings that were in reality cantilever units given additional strength by the use of interplane N-struts. The D VII was immensely strong, viceless and simple to fly, and also possessed very good high-altitude performance plus the ability to 'hang on its propeller'. The type entered large-scale production by Fokker and Albatros, and was greatly respected by Allied pilots. But by then the writing was on the wall for Germany: short of experienced pilots and fuel, the

Above: Radial engines were ideally suited to naval fighters such as the Boeing F4B-2 for their lightness, mechanical simplicity and reliability in comparison with inline engines and their associated liquid cooling system.

Right: The U.K's first carrierborne fighter, the Fairey Flycatcher surely retains the accolade of one of the ugliest fighters ever built, but served with great distinction at a time when the tactics and practice of carrierborne operations were being evolved in the early 1920s.

Above: The Gloster Gauntlet should have marked a radical improvement in British firepower, as it was designed for a battery of six guns (two in the fuselage and four in the wings). When it entered service, however, the battery had declined to the standard two guns.

Left: The Gladiator was evolved in succession to the Gauntlet, and in a way marked an interim measure towards fully-fledged monoplane fighters in possessing an enclosed cockpit, flaps, cantilever main landing gear legs and a four-gun battery.

German air arm could achieve little to stem the Allies' aerial tide in the closing stages of the war.

Other types were produced by the Germans in very small numbers, but these played only a minimal part in operations. Of these the most interesting are some of the naval fighters, particularly the Hansa-Brandenburg KDW and W 12 float-equipped biplanes, and the Hansa-Brandenburg W 29 float-equipped monoplane.

Germany's main partner in the Central Powers was Austria-Hungary, and though Austria-Hungary used mainly German aircraft, it produced some fighter designs of its own, most notably the Aviatik D I, often known as the Berg, and the Phönix-built Hansa-Brandenburg D I, often known as the 'Star-Strutter' in Allied circles for its unusual arrangement of interplane struts.

Italy was one of the Allied nations, fighting mostly against Austria-Hungary in northern Italy, and generally flew French fighters, though a small number of indigenously-designed Ansaldo A-1 Balilla biplane fighters did enter limited service. In the maritime war in the Adriatic, however, the Italians operated the Macchi M.5 and M.7 flying-boat fighters with twin forward-firing Fiat-Revelli machine-guns and remarkably good performance on the power of Isotta-Fraschini inline engines located between the high-set biplane wings to drive a pusher propeller.

The trauma inflicted on the economics and psyche of the Western world by 'The Great War' was so all-embracing that even today it cannot be adequately quantified. And foolish as it may now seem, there were very real expectations after the Armistice of 11 November 1918 that the world had just been through the 'war to end all wars'. So far as fighters (and indeed all other military) aircraft were concerned, the immediate consequences for the losers were a prohibition on the possession and development of military aircraft, and for the victors the cancellation of existing production contracts and the savage curtailment of further development as the huge wartime air forces were wound down to miniscule peacetime

Below: The Avia B-534 was a Czech biplane fighter broadly similar to the Gladiator. Powered by an 850-hp (634-kW) Avia-built Hispano-Suiza 12Y inline, the B-534 was built in versions with open and enclosed cockpits, and featured four fuselage-mounted machine-guns.

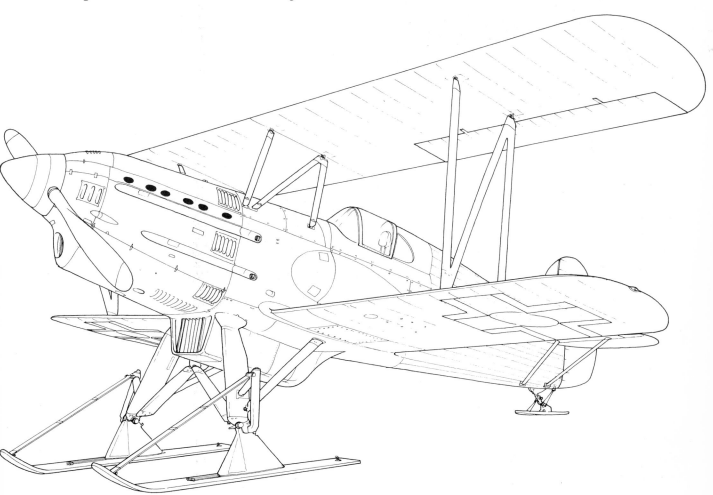

establishments. Throughout World War I, development, of both the technical and organisational types, had been undertaken on an *ad hoc* basis: this is hardly surprising as air forces were in their very earliest infancies in 1914, and the whole gamut of operational types have evolved within the context of operations in World War I. Much has been written since the savage retrenchment of the early 1920s about the inadvisability of the cuts imposed on the military. But so far as the air forces were concerned, it is arguable that the cuts in fact served a useful function in giving the authorities the chance to step back from operational matters, digest the organisational implications of the war, and begin to come to grips with the salient features of the new technology. They were therefore better placed to embark on a process of expansion to match the continued world problems that inevitably resurrected the spectre of global war.

Some new fighters did enter service in the years just after World War I, but these were generally the results of efforts in that war. The best example of this trend is the Nieuport 29, which began to enter French service in 1919 after development in 1918. This marked a departure for the manufacturer, for it was the first Nieuport design with an inline engine, a 300-hp (224-kW) Hispano-Suiza with its two Lamblin radiators carried inside the landing gear V-struts. The Nieuport 29 was fast, possessed an exceptional rate of climb, and was comparatively agile. More importantly, perhaps, the type served as the basis for racing and record-breaking aircraft that in turn helped the French to expand their technical capabilities and so pave the way for a later generation of fighters.

Much the same can be said of the standard U.S. fighter of the early 1920s, the MB-3 designed by Thomas-Morse but built by Boeing. This lacked the thoroughbred lines of the Nieuport 29, and

The Avia B-534 was produced in substantial numbers with alternative wheeled and ski landing gear, though the planned cantilever type was never installed. There was also a Bk-534 variant with an engine-mounted gun.

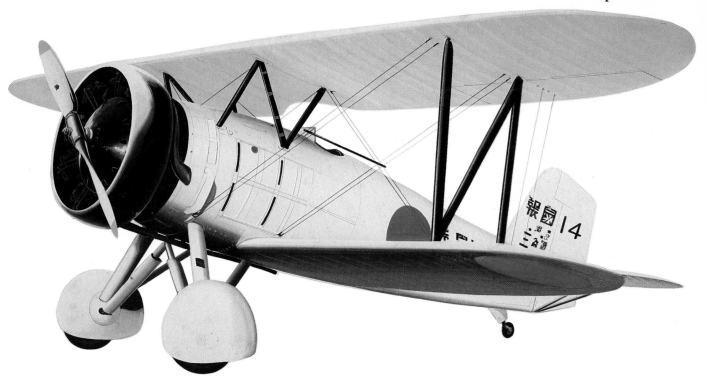

Above: The main carrierborne fighter in service with the Imperial Japanese Navy in the early and mid-1930s, the Nakajima A2N is a good example of the Japanese aero industry's penchant for adapting and developing Western designs, the A2N being based on the Japanese licence-built version of the Gloster Gambet. Power was provided by a 500-hp (373-kW) Nakajima Kotobuki radial, itself a development of the Bristol Jupiter, for a maximum speed of 183 mph (295 km/h), and the armament was a pair of Japanese-built Vickers guns.

to a certain extent must be considered the culmination of American efforts in World War I rather than the start of a new genre, but it is important as beginning U.S. mass manufacture of fighters, and as the fighter that introduced markedly heavier armament in the form of one 0.5-in (12.7-mm) and one 0.3-in (7.62-mm) machine-gun. Europe was slow to follow this lead, though various experimental fighters had featured heavier armament in World War I, and the Americans led consistently in weight of armament until the mid-1930s.

One field in which new development was inevitable was that of naval aircraft: aircraft-carriers had been pioneered by the British in the closing stages of World War I, and the early 1920s saw something of a 'boom' in the commissioning of such warships largely by the British and Americans. There had been naval fighters in World War I, but these had in general been landplanes operated by naval units for the protection of naval installations, or alternatively small flying-boats and float-equipped machines intended for coastal operations such as convoy escort and the harassment of the enemy's maritime reconnaissance flying-boats. Operations at sea from the moving deck of an aircraft-carrier presented different problems for the designers to overcome, and this led to the production of interim fighters such as the Beardmore W.B.III and Nieuport Nightjar, and then to the first full-production type, the Fairey Flycatcher in which outright performance was sacrificed to slow take-off and landing speed, great structural strength so that the aircraft could take the strains of heavy landings on the carriers, and compact overall dimensions (or indeed the ability to fold) so that the aircraft could be parked easily on the limited space of the deck or be struck down into the hangar. The Flycatcher was powered by a 425-hp (317-kW)

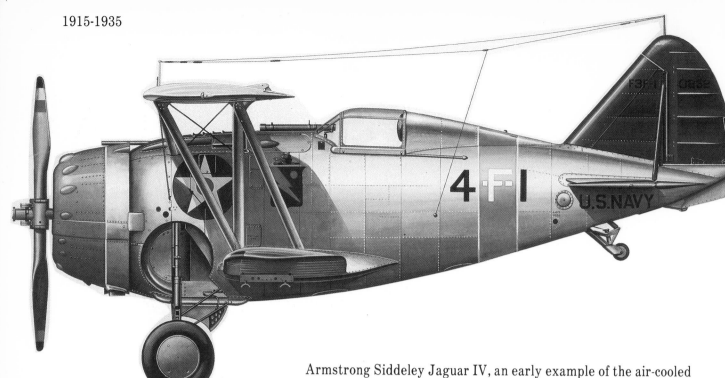

Naval air arms were generally more hesitant to come to grips with the new technology of the 1930s than air forces, and the Grumman F3F-1 marks a halfway point for the U.S. Navy. The biplane layout was retained, but here combined with an enclosed cockpit and retractable landing gear. Maximum speed was 237 mph (381 km/h). It had a 650-hp (485-kW) Pratt & Whitney R-1535 Twin Wasp radial.

Armstrong Siddeley Jaguar IV, an early example of the air-cooled radial piston engine that had begun to succeed to rotary engine in the closing stages of World War I, and which was now maturing into a reliable engine type without the weight of liquid cooling system required by inline engines, though only at the expense of considerably greater diameter so that the cylinders could be exposed to the cooling effects of the airflow.

In the U.S.A. a similar course of development resulted in the Boeing FB series, which went through FB-1 to FB-5 marks up to 1927, and the succeeding Curtiss F6C series of the later 1920s. These were powered by inline engines, in the form of a 425-hp (317-kW) Curtiss D-12 or 525-hp (392-kW) Packard 2A-1500 for the Boeing machine, and the 450-hp (336-kW) Curtiss D-12 for the Curtiss machine. Both aircraft types proved cost-effective in being part of a programme that saw their derivation from landplane fighters, the PW-9 and P-1 respectively. Just as importantly in the longer term, perhaps, these two types proved themselves the basis of a whole series of fighters used by the U.S. army and navy until well into the 1930s.

The Boeing series proceeded to the F2B and F3B, produced specifically to meet a fighter requirement for the navy's two great carriers U.S.S. *Lexington* and U.S.S. *Saratoga* commissioned in the second half of the 1920s. The F2B followed closely in the design steps of the FB, but was powered by the 425-hp Pratt & Whitney R-1340 Wasp radial, while the F3B used constant-chord rather than tapered wings, with the upper pair swept back. Next came the F4B based on the F3B but featuring a more compact overall design and an uprated 450-hp (336-kW) Wasp. The F4B was also developed for land use as the P-12 in a number of forms with Wasp engines rated at up to 575 hp (429 kW). The final expression of this series came with the land-based P-12E and the naval F4B-3 and F4B-4 with their fuselages built as metal semi-monocoque units instead of the previous metal tube structures covered with fabric.

Above: Extensively operated in the Spanish Civil War, the Fiat CR.32 was one of the most beautiful biplane fighters ever built, with adequate performance but sparkling agility.

Whereas the initial Boeing model progressed through the naval line, the Curtiss fighter evolved through the army line with the redoubtable and fondly-remembered Hawk series. First came the P-6 with the liquid-cooled Curtiss V-1570 Conqueror with a rating of 600 hp (448 kW), ultimately improved considerably in overall performance (especially ceiling and rate of climb) by the adoption of the Conqueror C with a supercharger in the P-6D. This was followed by the definitive P-6E with glycol rather than water coolant allowing the use of a smaller radiator that was relocated from the nose to a point under the fuselage between the cantilever main landing gear legs, which were themselves beautifully streamlined and fitted with spats for the wheels. The naval equivalent of the P-6 series was the F11C Goshawk, which was derived for the F6C but fitted with cantilever main landing gear legs and the 575-hp (429-kW) Wright R-1820 radial, a classic engine of great growth potential but then in its infancy. These Boeing and Curtiss fighters were produced only in comparatively small numbers, but were the

fighter mainstays of the U.S. forces in their important formative period.

The British too were beginning to press ahead with design of new fighters in the mid-1920s. First fruits of this renaissance were the Gloster Grebe and Armstrong Whitworth Siskin, both of them introduced in 1924. The philosophy behind the designs remained generally unaltered from World War I, though greater performance and reliability resulted from the use of the increasingly popular radial engine, the Armstrong Siddeley Jaguar in each case. The two fighters succeeded the Snipe, and were responsible for the introduction to British fighters of new features such as engine supercharging to maintain rated power at higher altitudes, radio and metal construction. The Grebe was succeeded in 1926 by another product from the drawing board of Henry Folland (designer of the S.E.5 and many other fighters up to the beautiful little Folland Gnat), the Gloster Gamecock powered by the 485-hp (362-kW) Bristol Jupiter radial. Next up the evolutionary ladder, by a small step, came the classic Bristol Bulldog. This appeared in 1929 and proved very popular in British service with the supercharged 530-hp (395-kW) Bristol Jupiter VIIF, and in export service with the more powerful Bristol Mercury IVS2 in a ring cowling.

Above: The Gladiator was technically obsolete by the standards of World War II's opening campaigns, but proved highly successful in secondary theatres such as Greece and North Africa where they were faced by Italian biplanes.

Right: One of the last biplane fighters to be designed, the Arado Ar 68 was an elegant design centred on a 690-hp (515-kW) Junkers Jumo 210 inline and clean lines including cantilever main landing gear legs. This is an example of the major production variant, the Ar 68E-1.

Apart from the refinements mentioned above, these fighters were little more than modestly updated expressions of World War I design concepts with more powerful engines. In the early 1930s the time was ripe for change, and the result was the superlative Hawker Fury I of 1931. As a company Hawker was successor to the now-defunct Sopwith, and the hallmark of the company's product line was a superb refinement of line and reversion to the liquid-cooled engine. The Fury I was powered by the 580-hp (433-kW) Rolls-Royce Kestrel IIS, and was the world's first fighter capable of 200 mph (322 km/h) in level flight. An equivalent model was produced for naval use as the Nimrod. A contemporary of these two single-seat fighters was the Hart two-seat light bomber with a more powerful variant of the Kestrel engine, and from this were evolved the Demon and Osprey two-seat land and naval fighters, the former with an armoured 'turret' for the gunner. This fighter line proved highly successful, and as late as 1937 Hawker introduced the refined Fury II, of which export versions were fitted with cantilever main landing gear legs.

The PZL P-11 was a notable Polish fighter evolved from the P-7 and retaining the characteristic gull-wing configuration. Powered by a 500-hp (373-kW) licence-built Bristol Mercury radial, the P-11 attained 242 mph (390 km/h) but was totally outclassed by the Bf 109 flown against it by the Germans in 1939.

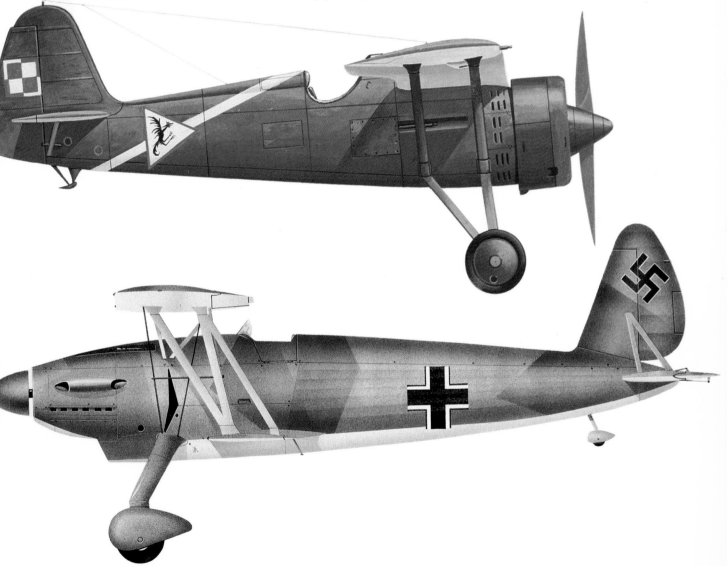

Above: Closely related to the Fury II fighter, the Hawker High-Speed Fury of 1933 was an experimental fighter powered by the 1,000-hp (746-kW) Rolls-Royce Goshawk evaporatively-cooled inline. The appearance of this elegant machine was later enhanced by the fitting of tapered outer wing panels.

The day of the biplane was really over, but the British did evolve two final efforts, the Gloster Gauntlet of 1935 and the Gloster Gladiator of 1937: the latter bridged the transition to multi-gun monoplane fighters with its enclosed cockpit, trailing-edge flaps and armament of four machine-guns, two of them located in the lower wings beyond the reach of the pilot.

The French turned to four-gun monoplane and sesquiplane fighters in the 1920s, the former epitomised by machines such as the Gourdou-Leseurre 32 and Wibault 7, and the latter by the elegant Nieuport-Delage 62. Then in the mid-1930s there appeared the extraordinarily angular Dewoitine D.500 series of low-wing monoplane fighters with massive landing gear arrangements. Poland followed a similar monoplane trend with the PWS-10 and then the striking-looking PZL P-7 and P-11 gull-winged fighters of the early and mid-1930s. Italy stuck to the biplane with the Fiat CR.30 and CR.32, and so too at first did the U.S.S.R. with a series of steadily developing biplanes that culminated with the superlative little Polikarpov I-15.

So what of the biplane fighter and its era, which came to its effective end in the mid-1930s with the introduction of the stressed-skin monoplane? The most important conclusion is that it was the biplane fighter which pioneered the technology and tactics of fighter combat. Through the medium of the biplane, the designers of the period were able to develop a combat aeroplane that combined a moderately powerful engine with a fairly light airframe of considerable structural strength: this produced a good power-to-weight ratio, resulting in a high rate of climb and modest acceleration. Thus from its earliest days the fighter was able to outperform its larger prey, notably two-seat tactical reconnaissance and artillery-spotter aircraft. This gave the fighter the operational benefit of being able to join combat only when the target was tactically disadvantaged, and of being able to break off the combat just as easily if this operational benefit was lost. The fact that the biplane wing cellule also offered considerable area within compact overall dimensions also promoted agility in the air, and this too was soon seen as an important operational advantage in its own right: it allowed the single-seat fighter to stalk its prey more effectively, and in combat allowed the pilot to bring his armament to bear more readily while retaining the capability to break away when tackled by another fighter.

The armament of these early aircraft was inevitably limited by

The incorporation of 'monoplane features' on the Gloster Gladiator not only improved performance, but helped pilots in the transitional phase to the new type of fighter entering service in the second half of the 1930s.

the weight which the fighter could lift and yet retain its margins of performance and agility. In effect this meant a pair of rifle-calibre machine-guns with their breeches located within reach of the pilot so that he could clear the all-too-common stoppages. Most fighter machine-guns were derived from substained-fire weapons designed for ground use, generally with air-cooling in place of the original water-cooling system, but with the erstwhile water jacket retained in lightened form to provide barrel rigidity. In the early days of fighters many authorities opined that a trainable machine-gun would provide the pilot with the best tactical weapon, but experience soon proved that the fixed gun was infinitely superior: the pilot could thus fly his aircraft into the right aiming position, knowing that the fire of his weapons would coincide with his natural line of sight, aided by a simple optical sight system (generally of the ring-and-bead type in a number of steadily improving types).

Above: Sporting dazzling colour schemes of various types, the Boeing P-26 'Peashooters' of the U.S. Army were very popular at a time when it was important for the service to maintain a high profile as one of the methods required to exert pressure on a parsimonious government for more modern equipment.

During the 1920s and early 1930s developments were introduced piecemeal, but the two major driving forces were the rapid development of powerful engines (of both the liquid-cooled inline and air-cooled radial types) and the adoption of stressed-skin metal construction based on aluminium alloys. At virtually a single stroke these combined with a host of lesser improvements (improved aerodynamics, retractable landing gear, high-lift devices, enclosed cockpit, etc.) to offer a quantum leap in performance. In turn this reduced and shortened the firing opportunities available to the fighter, and made it essential to increase the size of the fighter's battery not just to maintain hitting power but to increase it as a means of overcoming the greater structural and defensive strength of current bombers, now the most feared combat aircraft type and the fighter's most important prey. The fighter's offensive battery was also improved by the adoption of newer weapons, possessing greater reliability and higher rate of fire, aimed with the new type of reflector sight, itself soon supplemented and eventually overtaken by the gyro sight.

Below: The Boeing P-26A was phased out of U.S. service in 1940, this being an illustration of the type in the swansong of its service. However, P-26As in Chinese and Filipino service fought against the Japanese, suffering very heavy losses in the process.

1936-1953
The Monoplane Era

By the mid-1930s military aircraft had been overtaken in the vanguard of aeronautical development by a new breed of civil aircraft. Whereas the military and civilians alike had been content in the first half of the 1920s to consolidate the technology that emerged from World War I, with advances limited to experimental aircraft and considerable development of aero engines, the later 1920s and early 1930s had witnessed a rapid growth of civil aviation. Air travel was still extremely expensive, but with the growing acceptance of flight as a safe and realiable mode of transport, instead of just a fast one, there was a steadily burgeoning demand for such transport between the world's major countries, and even between the more important cities of large countries such as the U.S.A. Air mail helped to pave the way for this expansion of routes, while technical developments went a long way to meeting customer demand for comfort as well as speed and safety.

So while military aviation generally remained in the era of the 'stick-and-string' biplane, albeit translated in metal structures to increase airframe life and reduce the air forces' reliance on the high-quality timber that fell into such short supply during World War I, civil aviation began to forge ahead with a number of highly important technical developments. These are really a subject in their own right, and included such major innovations as fully cantilevered flying surfaces (for a considerable reduction in drag), semi-monocoque structures with stressed-skin covering (allowing the skinning over the airframe to bear much of the structural load, thereby allowing the internal structure to be lightened and also made more usable), all-metal structures (taking the semi-monocoque/stressed-skin concept one stage further for yet better performance as well as far greater airframe life), retractable landing gear units (for greatly reduced fuel consumption and higher speed, with the spin-off advantages of greater range for a given quantity of fuel), trailing-edge flaps (for reduced take-off and landing speeds with airframes of increasingly great weight), variable-pitch propellers (for blade performance optimised for all sectors of the flight regime rather than just one), enclosed cockpits (for increased crew comfort and therefore reduced crew fatigue) and much enhanced flight instruments (for safer operation of the aeroplane and also to promote accurate long-range navigation in adverse weather conditions). These and other features were incorporated piecemeal into a succession of civil aircraft, but the first machine to incorporate most of these features, and thus to become the world's

first 'modern' airliner, was the Boeing 247. This appeared in service during 1933, but within a year was supplanted by the more capable Douglas DC-2, forebear of the legendary DC-3. It is interesting to compare the DC-2 with a contemporary fighter such as the Gloster Gauntlet to see how far ahead the civil concept had forged. On the power of two 800-hp (597-kW) Wright SGR-1820 radials, the DC-2 could cruise for 1,000 miles (1,609 km) at 190 mph (306 km/h) after take-off at a loaded weight of 18,560 lb (8,419 kg) with 14 passengers in addition to the crew of three. The Gauntlet had not much less power, in the form of a 775-hp (578-kW) Bristol Mercury VIS radial, and could attain a maximum speed of 223 mph (359 km/h) at 15,000 ft (4,570 m), compared with the DC-2's 210 mph (338 km/h) at 8,000 ft (2,440 m), and attain a maximum range of 425 miles (684 km) after take-off at a loaded weight of 3,937 lb (1,200 kg). The fighter had usefully greater ceiling, but in other respects was in no way markedly superior in performance. Yet the airliner carried significantly greater payload on only double the power, despite the fact that the fighter marked a highpoint in the evolution of its type whereas the airliner was the starting point for a new breed. Great things were clearly in store.

The lower illustration shows the Ka-14 prototype with inverted gull wings.

So the time was ripe for a radical change in the fighter. The biplane had reached virtually its design limits in terms of structure and aerodynamics, and within a short time would clearly become

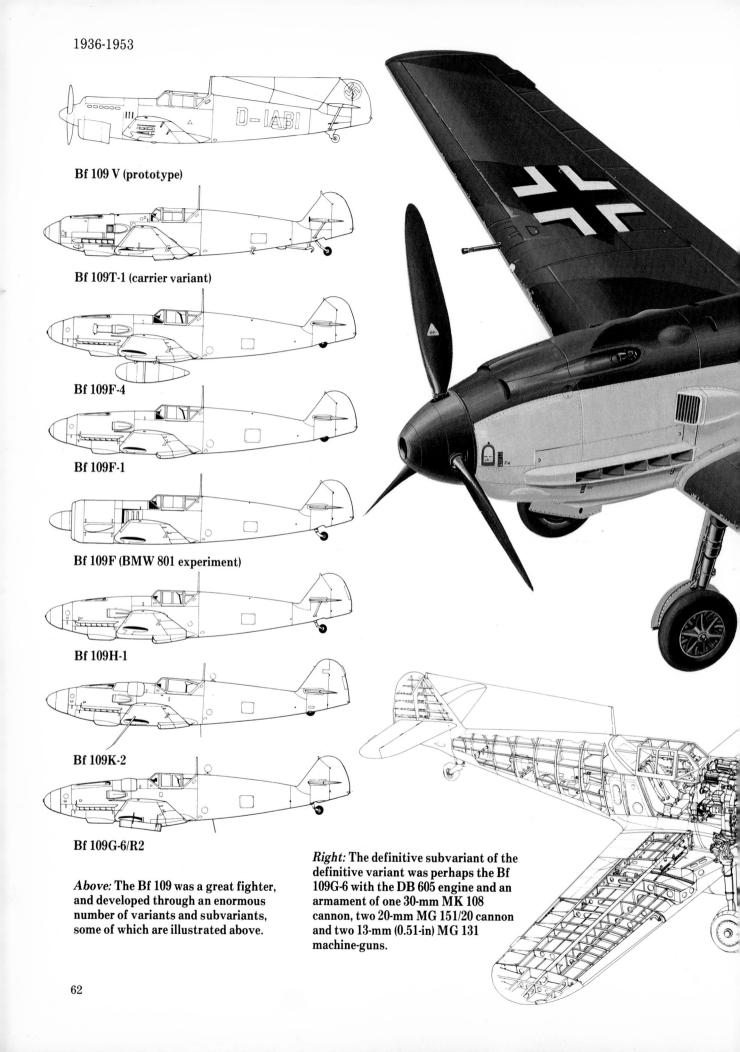

Bf 109 V (prototype)

Bf 109T-1 (carrier variant)

Bf 109F-4

Bf 109F-1

Bf 109F (BMW 801 experiment)

Bf 109H-1

Bf 109K-2

Bf 109G-6/R2

Above: The Bf 109 was a great fighter, and developed through an enormous number of variants and subvariants, some of which are illustrated above.

Right: The definitive subvariant of the definitive variant was perhaps the Bf 109G-6 with the DB 605 engine and an armament of one 30-mm MK 108 cannon, two 20-mm MG 151/20 cannon and two 13-mm (0.51-in) MG 131 machine-guns.

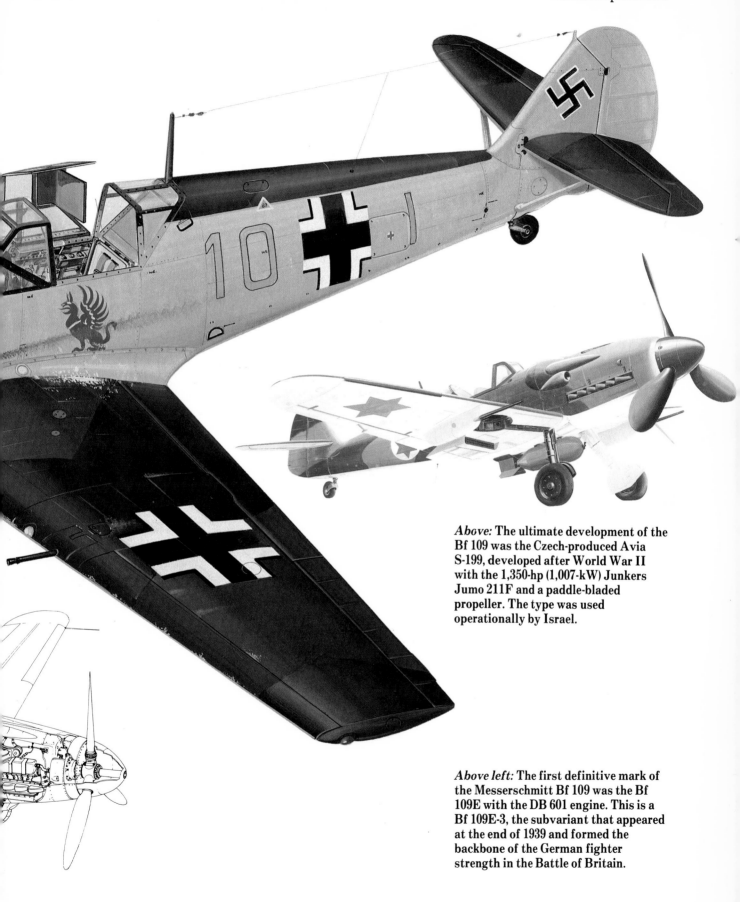

Above: The ultimate development of the Bf 109 was the Czech-produced Avia S-199, developed after World War II with the 1,350-hp (1,007-kW) Junkers Jumo 211F and a paddle-bladed propeller. The type was used operationally by Israel.

Above left: The first definitive mark of the Messerschmitt Bf 109 was the Bf 109E with the DB 601 engine. This is a Bf 109E-3, the subvariant that appeared at the end of 1939 and formed the backbone of the German fighter strength in the Battle of Britain.

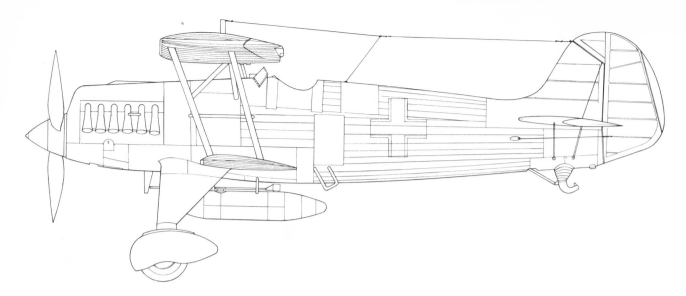

Above: One of Germany's last biplane fighters, the Heinkel He 51 was a worthy but by no means exceptional example of its type, and was still in very limited service at the beginning of World War II. The type was then used as an advanced trainer up to 1943.

incapable of catching, letting alone shooting down, the bombers beginning to appear with features pioneered on the new airliners. Inevitably there was resistance from those who believed that the fighter pilot could function effectively only in the open cockpit of a supremely agile aeróplane, but the inevitable change had already been foreshadowed by the service debut of interim monoplanes. Some of these, such as the French and Polish parasol and gull-wing fighters mentioned in the previous section, were already in service, but were restricted in performance by their continued need for bracing wires and/or struts, and by their continued reliance on fixed landing gear. Others showed a more far-sighted appearance, a typical example being the Boeing P-26 'Peashooter' that began to enter American service in 1933. This was the first U.S. Army fighter of all-metal construction and low-wing monoplane construction, but could attain only 234 mph (377 km/h) on the 570 hp (425 kW) of its Pratt & Whitney R-1340 Wasp radial because of its massively-faired fixed landing gear and the multiplicity of bracing wires needed by the wing, which was not of the cantilever type. The cockpit was open, and the armament was the standard U.S. combination of one 0.5-in (12.7-mm) and one 0.3-in (7.62-mm) Browning machine-gun.

It is interesting to compare the P-26 with a U.S. Navy equivalent, the Grumman FF-1. This was a biplane, but featured a fully-enclosed cockpit for the two crew, and also possessed landing gear whose main units retracted into the lower portion of the very bloated fuselage. The FF-1 was powered by a 600-hp (448-kW) Wright R-1820 radial, and returned a maximum speed of 201 mph (323 km/h) with an armament that comprised two fixed guns (either one 0.5-in and one 0.3-in weapon, or two 0.3-in weapons), plus a trainable 0.3-in gun for the rear-seater and two 116-lb (53-kg) bombs. This basic design philosophy was perpetuated in a single-seat derivative, the Grumman F2F of 1935 and its development, the F3F: powered by a 650-hp (485-kW) Pratt & Whitney R-1535 Twin Wasp radial, the F2F could touch 233 mph (375 km/h).

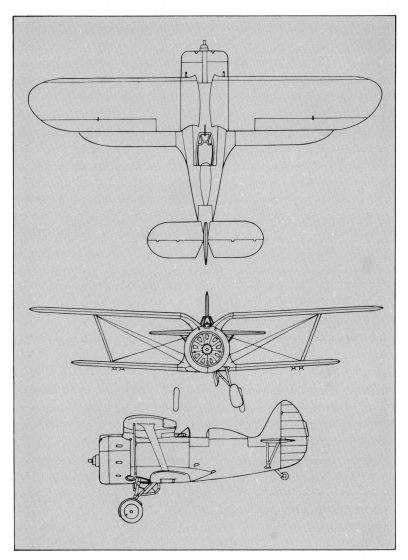

Right: The ultimate development of the attractive Polikarpov I-15 biplane fighter was the I-153, which introduced retractable landing gear to boost performance. With a 1,000-hp (746-kW) Shvetsov M-62 radial, the I-153 attained 267 mph (430 km/h) and carried an armament of four 7.62-mm (0.3-in) machine-guns, supplemented on occasion by six RS-82 82-mm (3.2-in) rockets carried under the wings.

Interesting as these aircraft were, they could not stave off the development of genuine low-wing monoplane fighters with retractable landing gear and a significantly heavier armament. The distinction of being the first country to introduce such a fighter goes to the U.S.S.R., which had laboured industriously and often effectively to develop aircraft and aircraft weapons industries in the 1920s and early 1930s. This epoch-making fighter was the Polikarpov I-16, which began to enter service in 1934 at a time when the Western world was happy to remain in ignorance of the U.S.S.R.'s growing strength and capabilities. The I-16 was a capable but not decisive aeroplane, but in the design for this four-gun fighter were blended for the first time in such an aircraft retractable landing gear, a low-set cantilever monoplane wing, a well-streamlined fuselage and, in later versions, an enclosed cockpit and variable-pitch propeller. Powered by a 700-hp (522-kW) M-25 radial, the I-16 attained 249 mph (400 km/h), and in later marks went on to feature an impressive cannon armament. The U.S.A. went along a similar path with the Seversky P-35, which entered limited service from 1937, but the pace of development then pushing ahead in

Europe meant that the P-35 was obsolete even as it was entering service.

First off the mark was Germany, where an ambitious programme of military development had provided both the political incentive and the financial muscle for Germany's designers to move rapidly ahead. The newly-revealed Luftwaffe had started life with biplane fighters such as the Arado Ar 68 and Heinkel He 51, good examples of the biplane fighter in the evensong of its career, but the need to build an overwhelmingly strong tactical air force to support Germany's new doctrines of Blitzkrieg warfare meant emphasis first on quality and then on quantity. Prototypes were produced of several types, but the clear winner was the Messerschmitt Bf 109, many of whose design features had been pioneered on the highly successful Bf 108 Taifun touring and liaison aeroplane. In common with just about every fighter of its era, the Bf 109 was eventually employed as a maid-of-all-work fighter in roles as diverse as high-altitude interception to low-altitude fighter-bomber work, but first flew in 1935 as an air-superiority fighter planned for heavy weapons and a powerful engine as soon as the basic concept had been proved. Only a relatively small fuel load was envisaged, and it was decided that performance could be optimised by the use of small wings, whose heavy loading could be offset (to provide comparatively modest take-off and landing speeds) by the combination of leading-edge slots and trailing-edge flaps. The fuselage was slim and the cockpit cramped, this emphasis being carried into the landing gear, which was of narrow track with the main units hinged under the fuselage to retract into the lower surfaces of the wings. Both the cockpit and the landing gear were later to become the major disadvantages of the Bf 109.

Perhaps inevitably at such a time of transition, initial reactions to

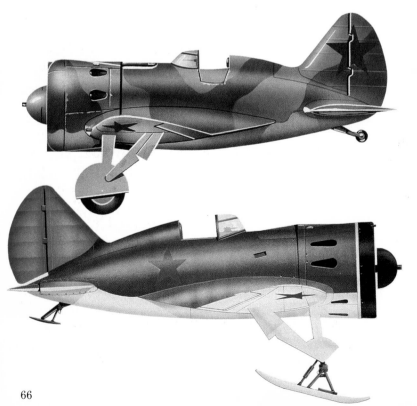

Left: The Polikarpov I-16 has the distinction of being the world's first modern monoplane fighter to have entered service. The type was designed at much the same time as the I-15, and was extensively developed with radial engines ranging from the 450-hp (336-kW) M-22 to the 1,000-hp (746-kW) M-63, producing maximum speeds from 224 to 326 mph (360 to 525 km/h). Various machine-gun and cannon combinations were installed, but by 1941 the I-16 was hopelessly outclassed by German fighters and destroyed in vast numbers in the air and on the ground.

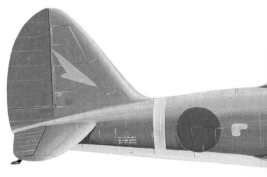

Above: The U.K's first modern monoplane fighter was the Hawker Hurricane Mk I with the great Rolls-Royce Merlin engine and, initially, a two-blade fixed-pitch wooden propeller.

Below: The Imperial Japanese Army's equivalent to the navy's A5M was the Nakajima Ki-27 'Nate'. This is an example of the definitive Ki-27b with aerodynamic improvements to increase speed to 286 mph (460 km/h). The armament remained light, at just two 7.7-mm (0.303-in) machine-guns.

the new fighter were mixed. But the prototypes soon revealed outstanding performance and adequate handling, soon winning the confidence of previously sceptical pilots and commanders. The type began to enter service in 1937 as the Bf 109B with the Junkers Jumo 210 engine and an armament of three 7.9-mm (0.31-in) machine-guns, later increased to five weapons of the same calibre. The Bf 109 was blooded in the Spanish Civil War, and even in its earlier forms showed itself capable of besting the I-16, which had hitherto reigned supreme. But the Bf 109B was little more than a pre-production type, and was soon superseded by the more definitive Bf 109D, which started life with the 680-hp (507-kW) Jumo 210D and a speed of 280 mph (450 km/h) before reaching an interim maturity the 1,000-hp (746-kW) Daimler-Benz DB600 and a speed of 305 mph (490 km/h). The armament was also revised, and now included a 20-mm cannon firing through the propeller hub. With these early models, however, both the manufacturer and the operating service had been feeling their way into the new technology and the tactics to go with it. The first genuine mass-production version of the Messerschmitt single-seat fighter was thus the Bf 109E of 1938, which introduced the 1,100-hp (821-kW) DB601 engine with direct fuel injection rather than a carburettor: this allowed the fighter to undertake the negative-g manoeuvres (such as a sharp dive straight from level flight without a preliminary half-roll) impossible for carburettor-fitted fighters unless the pilot was prepared to have his engine cut out. By 1939 and the outbreak of World War II the 'Emil' was the standard fighter of the German fighter arm, and its armament was either four 7.9-mm machine-guns (two synchronised and two unsynchronised) or the synchronised pair of machine-guns and a pair of unsynchronised 20-mm MG FF cannon in the wings outboard of the propeller disc.

Even as the Bf 109 was entering widespread service, there were air arms that disagreed vehemently with the design philosophy epitomised by the German fighter. Two such were the Imperial Japanese army and navy, which envisaged that fighter combat would continue to require a light wing loading for maximum agility. The Japanese did not sacrifice performance outright, but instead placed emphasis on the development of what can perhaps be called a hybrid fighter concept with much of the advanced Western monoplane's performance allied to the agility of the biplane: this was achieved through the use of a light but only moderately powerful radial engine, a comparatively large wing and a lightweight structure allied to features such as an open cockpit, fixed landing gear and light machine-gun armament, which was made effective in Japanese tactical thinking by close engagement to make every round count. As part of this concept the Japanese refused to have any truck with developments, such as armour protection and self-sealing fuel tanks, that were becoming increasingly common in Western fighters. To Japanese thinking these added weight to no real purpose, thereby requiring additional power from an engine that in turn entailed a larger and heavier airframe, etc., in an upward spiral that steadily degraded performance and agility.

This all had the effect of encouraging the design of simple fighters whose maintenance was that much more practical within the confines, both logistical and physical, of the forward airfields envisaged in remote areas by both the army and navy, and in the navy's aircraft-carriers. The results of this thinking were the superlative if short-sighted Mitsubishi A5M, called the Type 96 Carrier Fighter by the navy and dubbed 'Claude' by the Allies in World War II, and the slightly later Nakajima Ki-27, called the Type 97 Fighter by the army and dubbed 'Nate' by the Allies.

The A5M entered service in 1937 with the 630-hp (470-kW) Nakajima Kotobuki radial, and through the use of lightweight structure (incorporating the standard Japanese armament of just two rifle-calibre machine-guns) and a highly polished finish over flush riveting achieved the very creditable maximum speed of 252 mph (406 km/h). The A5M was undoubtedly the world's finest carrierborne fighter at the time of its introduction, and was widely used in the Sino-Japanese War, as was the Ki-27 that followed two years later as a result of an indifferently-run development programme. In basic configuration and armament the Ki-27 was very similar to the A5M, but was powered by the 710-hp (530-kW) Nakajima Ha-1 radial for a maximum speed of 292 mph (470 km/h). If anything, the Ki-27 was yet more agile in the air than the A5M, but was faced with the tactical problem of tackling land-based fighters with higher overall performance than those which the A5M would have to engage.

The implications of these fighters, and of the many other advanced Japanese aircraft deployed in the Sino-Japanese war, should have rung alarm bells in the defence ministries of all countries threatened by Japan's expansionist dreams, but failed to do so: the Western powers rested confident in the smug belief that Japan was merely an inferior copyist of Western ideas, and was thus always behind the times in technological development. Japan was indeed never loath to seize on Western developments: these were not slavishly copied in a second-rate fashion, however, but carefully and imaginatively blended into an overall concept of Japanese origins. In the longer term the Japanese fighter concept was proved to be wrong, but in the short term it provided the imperial army and navy with fighters well able to dominate the skies over their imaginatively used ground and naval forces. Their simplicity was also an advantage on forward airfields.

In other parts of the aeronautical world designers were now beginning to come to realistic grips with the concept of the modern monoplane fighter, though the capabilities of the new fighters that began to appear were widely different in reflection of factors as diverse as the basic national design philosophies and the availability of suitable powerplant types.

The breathing space bought by the introduction of the Gloster Gladiator allowed the development in the U.K. of the Hawker Hurricane and Supermarine Spitfire, both of them destined to become decisive weapons in World War II. The earlier of the two was the Hurricane, designed under the leadership of Sidney Camm,

Bf 110A-0

Bf 110C-4/B

Bf 110D-3

Bf 110G-4C/R3

Above: **Designed as a bomber destroyer, the Bf 110 was more successfully used for reconnaissance and then as a night-fighter in several marks.**

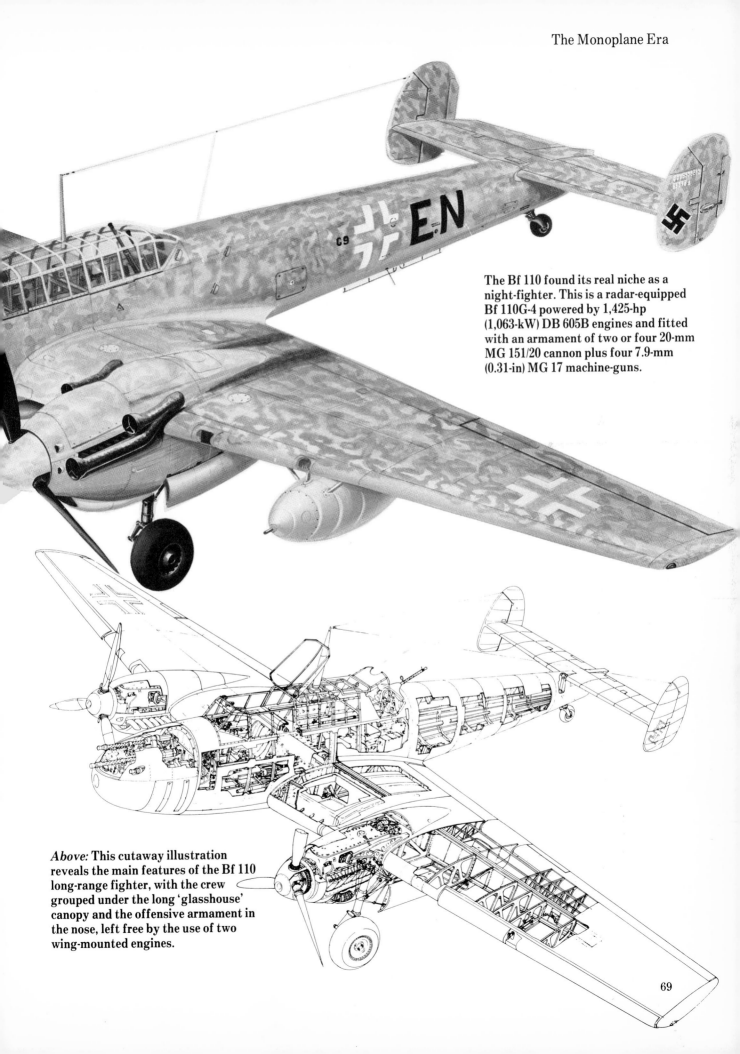

The Bf 110 found its real niche as a
night-fighter. This is a radar-equipped
Bf 110G-4 powered by 1,425-hp
(1,063-kW) DB 605B engines and fitted
with an armament of two or four 20-mm
MG 151/20 cannon plus four 7.9-mm
(0.31-in) MG 17 machine-guns.

Above: This cutaway illustration
reveals the main features of the Bf 110
long-range fighter, with the crew
grouped under the long 'glasshouse'
canopy and the offensive armament in
the nose, left free by the use of two
wing-mounted engines.

that classic fighter designer already responsible for the Fury and with such machines as the Typhoon, Tempest, Sea Fury and Hunter ahead of him. With this first-generation monoplane fighter, Camm opted for a fairly conservative design approach, so while contemporaries were moving into stressed-skin metal construction the Hawker fighter retained a primary structure of metal tube covered with fabric. This meant that while the Hurricane lacked the development potential of more advanced fighters, in the shorter term it could be brought into production and operational maturity that much more rapidly. It is also worth noting that the Hurricane had an unquantifiable 'something' about it: by the Battle of Britain in 1940 the Hurricane was definitely inferior in most objective features to the Bf 109, yet emerged as by far the most successful fighter of that battle, and then went on to build an enviable second career as a potent fighter-bomber with heavier inbuilt and disposable armament.

The origins of the Hurricane can be traced to the Fury biplane via Camm's scheme for a Fury monoplane powered by the 660-hp (492-kW) Rolls-Royce Goshawk steam-cooled engine. This notion was abandoned when the 1,000-hp (746-kW) Rolls-Royce P.V.12 was evolved from the company's experience with the 'R' engines used in the final examples of the Supermarine racing floatplanes that had won the Schneider Trophy for the U.K. The P.V.12 entered production as the Merlin, perhaps the single most important aero engine used by the Allies in World War II. With the extra power promised by the new engine, Camm was able to revise his ideas and produce the Hurricane with extreme structural strength, wide-track inward-retracting main landing gear and a battery of four 0.303-in (7.7-mm) machine-guns in each wing. The Hurricane first flew in November 1935 on the 1,190 hp (888 kW) provided by the Merlin C, and was clearly a winner: agility was excellent, and the top speed was a highly respectable 315 mph (507 km/h). Just as importantly, the rate of climb and ceiling were impressive, and it was these two features that became significant when the U.K.'s

Right: The Curtiss Hawk 75 was the export version of the P-36, finding a ready market in the dire days of 1939 and 1940 when the poorly prepared democracies faced the threat of totalitarian invasion and found in the Hawk 75 an adequate fighter that could be produced rapidly in large numbers.

Below: Numerically the most significant French fighter of 1939, the Morane-Saulnier M.S.406 had a useful armament, thanks to the installation of a 20-mm *moteur canon* as well as two 7.5-mm (0.295-in) machine-guns, but was obsolete in terms of performance.

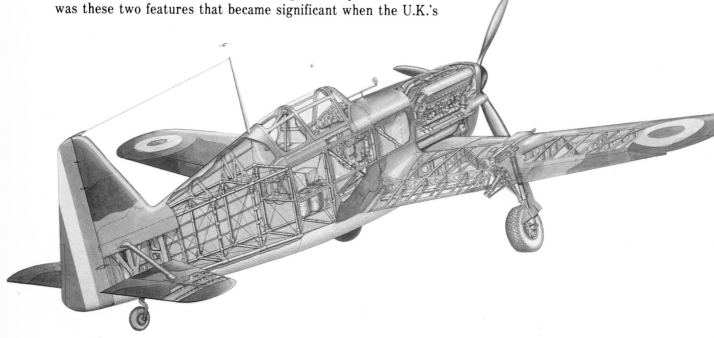

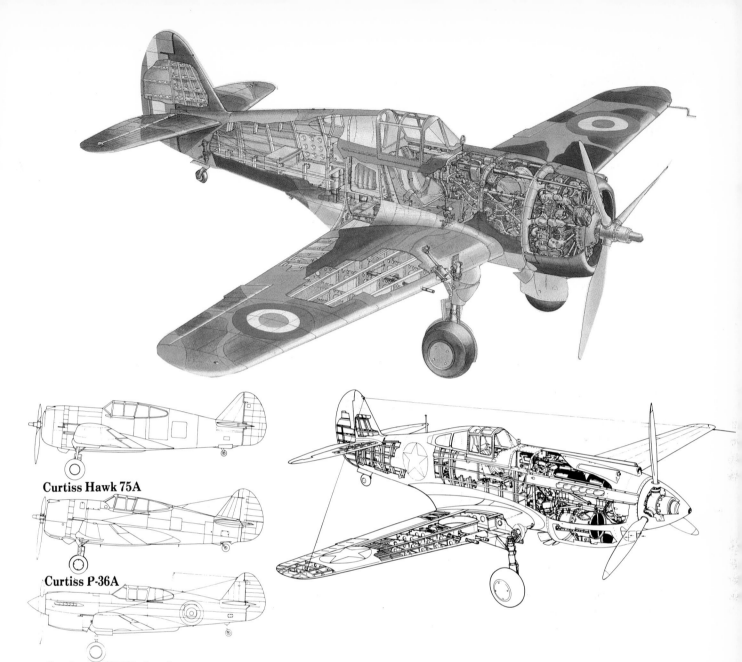

Curtiss Hawk 75A

Curtiss P-36A

Curtiss P-40E Warhawk

Curtiss P-40N Warhawk

Above: The family relationship of the P-36 and P-40 is clear from this small selection of variants.

Above right: The Curtiss P-40 was typical of fighter design in the late 1930s, with the cockpit running into a dorsal fairing that reduced rearward vision, and a trim radiator installation. One unusual feature, inherited from the P-36, was the rearward retraction of the main landing gear legs.

chain of early warning radar stations entered service. No longer did fighters such as the initial Hurricane Mk I, which began to enter service in November 1937, need to patrol at high altitude in air for an enemy that might or might not come, in the process consuming precious fuel and wasting valuable engine and airframe hours while their pilots became increasingly fatigued: instead they could wait on the ground until the radar warned of an approaching foe, then take off and attain the tactical advantages of higher altitude using their much improved climb performance. Naturally enough, given the fact that this was a period of both development and expansion, the capabilities of this fighter were improved as rapidly as possible: for example, the Hurricane Mk I entered service with a fixed-pitch two-blade wooden propeller for its 1,225-hp (914-kW) Merlin II, and could attain a maximum speed of 310 mph (499 km/h) at 17,000 ft (5,180 m); by 1940 the current model was using the 1,245-hp (929-kW) Merlin III driving a more advanced constant-speed three-blade metal propeller, and this allowed the Hurricane a maximum speed of

Left: The Fiat CR.42 Falco was the final expression of Italy's long adherence to the biplane fighter concept, and for lack of a suitable replacement was forced to soldier on, largely as a ground-attack aircraft, while completely obsolete.

Right: In most respects the Macchi C.200 Saetta was an admirable fighter, but lack of a suitably powerful engine provided only indifferent performance, a factor exacerbated by light armament.

316 mph (509 km/h) at 17,750 ft (5,410 m). More importantly, rate of climb and ceiling were also improved by the use of the constant-speed propeller.

The Spitfire was a more advanced aeroplane in concept, and was thus more difficult to get into mass production though it offered the longer-term advantages of greater 'stretch', or development potential. R.J. Mitchell, the designer of the Spitfire, had developed many of his design ideas on the Supermarine Schneider Trophy racers, but there was little if any direct relationship between these floatplanes and the supremely elegant Spitfire. Like the Hurricane, the Spitfire was intended from the start to be powered by the Merlin and use the same battery of eight machine-guns, located as a quartet in each wing outside the propeller disc and designed to converge into a concentrated pattern some 400 yards (365-m) ahead of the aeroplane. But by comparison with the Hurricane the Spitfire was of more 'state of the art' stressed-skin metal monocoque construction with elliptical wings married to an oval-section fuselage and curved tail surfaces all mounted on unfortunately narrow-track main landing gear units that retracted outward to lie in the undersurfaces of the wings, just like those of the Bf 109. This meant that while the Hurricane and other fighters with wide-track landing gear were able to use rough fields without difficulty, the Bf 109 and Spitfire were not so blessed and suffered a greater number of landing accidents. The Spitfire made its first flight in March 1936, but began to enter service as the Spitfire Mk I only in June 1938 because of the delays in establishing the production programme for this advanced aeroplane. Thereafter the pace of deliveries increased rapidly, but by the time of the Battle of Britain in mid-1940 the Hurricane was still numerically more important. The Spitfire Mk I used the 1,225-hp Merlin II with a two-blade fixed-pitch wooden propeller, and its optimum rate of climb ws 2,530 ft (771 m) per minute at 11,000 ft (3,355 m). The Spitfire Mk IIA had the 1,235-hp Merlin XII with a three-blade constant-speed metal propeller, and its optimum rate of climb was 3,025 ft (922 m) per minute at 12,800 ft

Below: Fitted with the 1,475-hp (1,100-kW) Fiat RA.1050 Tifone (licence-built DB 605A) engine and carrying an armament of two 20-mm and two 12.7-mm (0.5-in) guns, the Macchi C.205V Veltro was a match for any 1943 fighter, with a maximum speed of 401 mph (645 km/h) but the agility of the earlier C.200. Only a few were built before Italy's capitulation.

Below: Even fighter pilots have to learn their flying skills from the bottom up, and start their training in simple aircraft without vices.

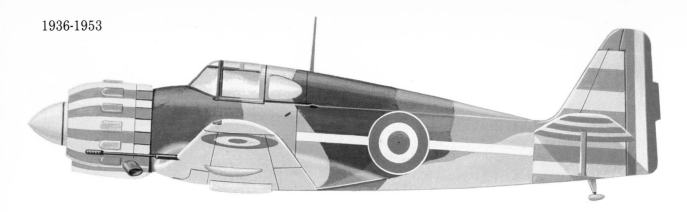

(3,900 m). The times to reach 20,000 and 30,000 ft (6,094 and 9,145 m) were 9 minutes 25 seconds and 22 minutes 25 seconds respectively for the Mk I, and 7 minutes and 13 minutes 40 seconds for the Mk IIA, while the service ceilings of the two marks were 31,900 ft (9,725 m) and 37,600 ft (11,460 m). Given the fact that the power available to each model was roughly similar, the differences in climb rate and ceiling were very large, and attributable mostly to the different propellers. Performance increments of the same nature were available to other fighters adopting the same type of propeller technology and supercharged engines able to maintain rated power to higher altitudes.

The French were off the mark at about the same time as the British, but lost much through the diversification of effort in a poorly co-ordinated programme that saw the development of too many engine and airframe prototypes in a virtual chaos that spread right through the French aircraft industry and air force. In the fighter field the most significant machines were the Morane-Saulnier M.S. 406, the Bloch M.B.151 and the Dewoitine D.520. The M.S.406 was a workmanlike first-generation monoplane fighter powered by an 860-hp (642-kW) Hispano-Suiza 12Y liquid-cooled engine, but was limited in basic performance and growth potential by its indifferent powerplant and outmoded construction, which used fabric or plywood/metal covering over a core structure of metal. The armament comprised two 7.5-mm (0.295-in) rifle-calibre machine-guns in the wings and one 20-mm cannon firing through the propeller hub, and the maximum speed was 301 mph (485 km/h). The prototype first flew in August 1935, and by the outbreak of World War II in September 1939 the M.S.406 was France's most important fighter. The M.B.151 was a better machine, with a more modern structure and powered by a 1,000-hp (746-kW) Gnome-Rhône 14N radial engine. The powerplant installation was not very neat, and the M.B.151 was armed with either four rifle-calibre machine-guns, or two such guns and two 20-mm cannon. Firepower

Above: **The Bloch M.B.150 series provided France's best balance of fighter numbers and capability in 1940. This is an M.B.151 with a 1,080-hp (806-kW) rather than 920-hp (686-kW) Gnome-Rhône 14N radial for a maximum speed raised from 298 to 323 mph (480 to 520 km/h). The armament was either two 20-mm cannon and two 7.5-mm (0.295-in) machine-guns, or four machine-guns.**

Below: **The Boulton Paul Defiant failed because of the inherent limitations of its tactical concept — and this concept failed as soon as the German fighter pilots realised that this was not an agile single-seat fighter with eight fixed machine-guns, but rather a clumsy two-seater with a four-gun turret. Maximum speed of the Defiant Mk I was 303 mph (488 km/h) on a 1,030-hp (768-kW) Merlin III.**

In common with other Italian fighters of its period, the Reggiane Re.2000 was crippled in operational terms by its poor armament and lack of power.

was greater than that of the M.S.406, therefore, and the M.B.151 was also more agile as well as having slightly better performance. This initial model was succeeded by the M.B.152 with uprated engine and slight improvements in performance, including a maximum speed of 320 mph (515 km/h). The best fighter to have entered French service by the date of France's capitulation in June 1940, however, was the trim D.520. This first flew in October 1938, but only small numbers had been produced before France's fall. These served with distinction and were later complemented by additional production, though plans for radically improved models

Below: Fitted with the 1,150-hp (858-kW) DB 601A, the Falco became the Re.2001 and an altogether more capable aircraft with a maximum speed of 351 mph (565 km/h).

with different engines were never realised. The basic fighter was powered by the 910-hp (679-kW) Hispano-Suiza 12Y, reached a maximum speed of 329 mph (530 km/h) nd carried an armament of four rifle-calibre machine-guns and one 20-mm cannon in the *moteur canon* position widely admired by the French.

While the Japanese appreciated the agility and the total 'fightability' of the biplane, they had been professional enough to realise that the day of the biplane had closed. However, the Italians pushed ahead with this obsolete type, their experience in the Spanish Civil War seeming to have confirmed that the well-handled biplane was still supreme. What Italy's dismal operational analysis had failed to take into account was the fact that the Italian fighters flying on the Nationalist side were faced with only a miscellany of indifferent types flown by the Republican side's poor-quality fighter pilot force. So from the Fiat CR.32 that had performed creditably in

Below: **The Supermarine Spitfire Mk II began to enter service in 1940 with the 1,175-hp (876-kW) Merlin XII and an armament of eight 0.303-in (7.7-mm) machine-guns (Spitfire Mk IIA) or two 20-mm cannon and four machine-guns (Spitfire Mk IIB). It was this nicely developed variant that inaugurated Fighter Command's growing offensive over northern Europe in 1941.**

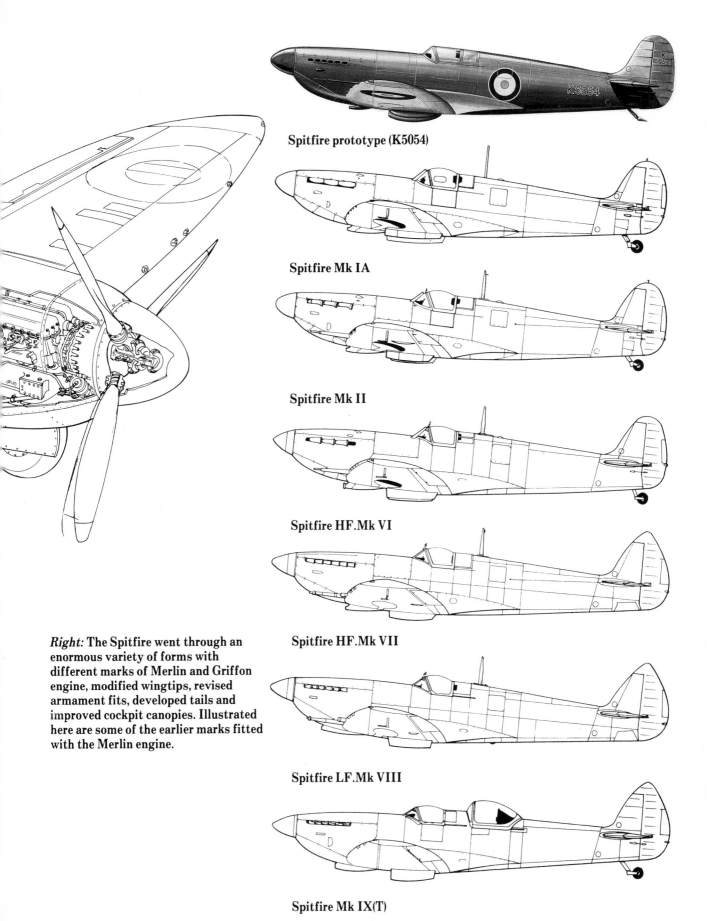

Spitfire prototype (K5054)

Spitfire Mk IA

Spitfire Mk II

Spitfire HF.Mk VI

Spitfire HF.Mk VII

Spitfire LF.Mk VIII

Spitfire Mk IX(T)

Right: The Spitfire went through an enormous variety of forms with different marks of Merlin and Griffon engine, modified wingtips, revised armament fits, developed tails and improved cockpit canopies. Illustrated here are some of the earlier marks fitted with the Merlin engine.

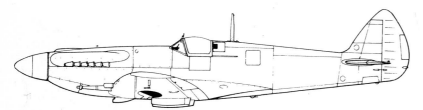

Spitfire Mk XII

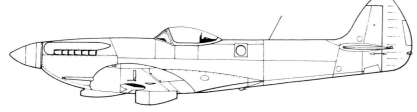

Spitfire FR.Mk XIV

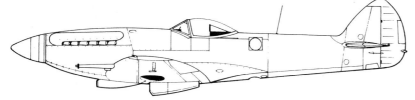

Spitfire FR.Mk XVIII

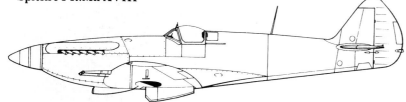

Spitfire F.Mk 21

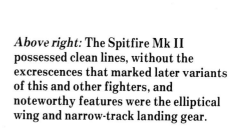

Above right: The Spitfire Mk II possessed clean lines, without the excrescences that marked later variants of this and other fighters, and noteworthy features were the elliptical wing and narrow-track landing gear.

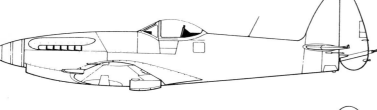

Spitfire F.Mk 22

Left: As these illustrations reveal, the Spitfire family was also developed as the Seafire naval fighter, which had a counterpart to the new-generation Spiteful in the Seafang, both fitted with laminar flow wings.

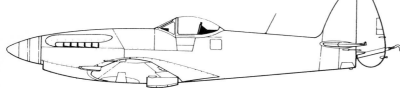

Below: Some 3,923 Spitfire Mk Vs were produced, this being a low-altitude variant with clipped tips to increase roll rate.

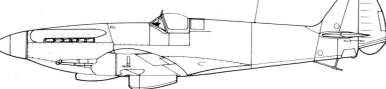

Seafire F.Mk 45

the atypical conditions of the Spanish Civil War the Italians developed the ultimate biplane fighter in the form of the Fiat CR.42 Falco. This first flew in 1939 and began to enter service in 1940, remaining in Italian service until the capitulation of 1943. Powered by an 840-hp (627-kW) Fiat A.74 radial in a very neat installation, the CR.42 had fixed but well streamlined landing gear, a very strong wing cellule with interplane W-struts, and a high level of agility. Speed was quite good given the fact that the type was a biplane with an open cockpit, 267 mph (430 km/h) being attained at medium altitudes, but the armament was indifferent, comprising just a pair of machine-guns, though these were at least of the moderately powerful 12.7-mm (0.5-in) Breda-SAFAT type and thus more effective than rifle-calibre weapons.

The Italians did not totally ignore the monoplane but, like the Japanese, saw the future as lying with a hybrid concept that married part of the advanced monoplane's performance with most of the biplane's agility. Inevitably this resulted in fighters that failed to live up to their promise, and this tendency was often reinforced

Above: The cockpit of the Spitfire Mk II.

Below: The Seafire Mk IIC was the first Seafire built as such, but was based on the original Seafire Mk IB (Spitfire Mk VB navalised with a retractable arrester hook) with strengthening for catapult launches and fitted with a 'Universal' wing.

by the indifferent power of the engines available from Italian domestic manufacture. Though Italy had produced excellent liquid-cooled engines in the 1920s, and some extremely promising record-breaking engines of the same variety in the 1930s, the balance had swung towards the lighter weight of the air-cooled radial which had then been developed to only modest power ratings. This combination of insufficiently powerful radial and virtually non-existent inline engines bedevilled Italian fighter design right through the late 1930s and early 1940s, and was alleviated only with the import of German engines and then their production under licence in Italy.

The first Italian monoplane fighter was the Fiat G.50 Freccia, which was first flown in February 1937 and evaluated in the Spanish Civil War before the G.50bis was authorised for full production: one of the modifications made as a result of the Spanish experience was reversion from an enclosed to an open cockpit, and the powerplant was the same A.74 radial as used in the CR.42. The G.50bis was indeed agile, but its maximum speed was a mere 292 mph (470 km/h) and the armament remained the standard pair of 12.7-mm machine-guns. A near-contemporary was the Macchi C.200 Saetta, designed by Mario Castoldi. This capable designer had been responsible for the racing floatplanes that had contested the Schneider Trophy's last races against the products of R.J. Mitchell, and the Saetta bore the same relationship to these racers as the Spitfire to the S.5 and S.6 floatplanes. The Saetta was again powered by the A.74 radial, fitted with two 12.7-mm machine-guns and reverted from an enclosed to an open cockpit to satisfy pilot demand, but was potentially a devastating fighter: even on its modest 840 hp it could attain 308 mph (495 km/h), yet was both sturdy and manoeuvrable.

Produced against the same specification as the Saetta, the Reggiane Re.2000 Falco I bore a striking similarity to the Seversky P-35 of American design, and though it retained the standard two heavy machine-guns it had an enclosed cockpit and a 1,000-hp Piaggio PXI radial for a maximum speed of 336 mph (540 km/h). Only a few were produced for the Italian navy, most production examples being exported. Like the other Italian monoplane fighters of its generation, the Falco I was agile and possessed a high initial rate of climb, but began to fail badly at heights above 15,000 ft (4,570 m) for lack of a usefully-supercharged engine.

American fighter design was in the doldrums during this period, the only important developments being the P-35 already mentioned (together with its unsuccessful derivative, the P-43 Lancer) and the Curtiss P-36 that began to enter service in 1938 with the 1,050-hp (783-kW) Pratt & Whitney R-1830 Twin Wasp radial for a top speed of 300 mph (493 km/h). This was a successful export offering (with the designations Mohawk and Hawk 75) and went through a series of marks with increasingly heavy rifle-calibre machine-gun armament, but is important primarily as the precursor of the Curtiss P-40 Warhawk. This was developed as an inline-engined derivative of the P-36, and was one of several interesting designs to a 1937 U.S. Army specification issued in response to the perceived

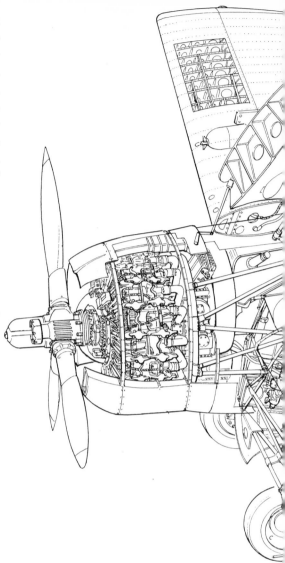

Above: The Grumman F4F was the U.S. Navy's first effective monoplane fighter designed for carrierborne operations, and a notably sturdy aeroplane well able to withstand combat damage and still remain capable of using its own substantial firepower.

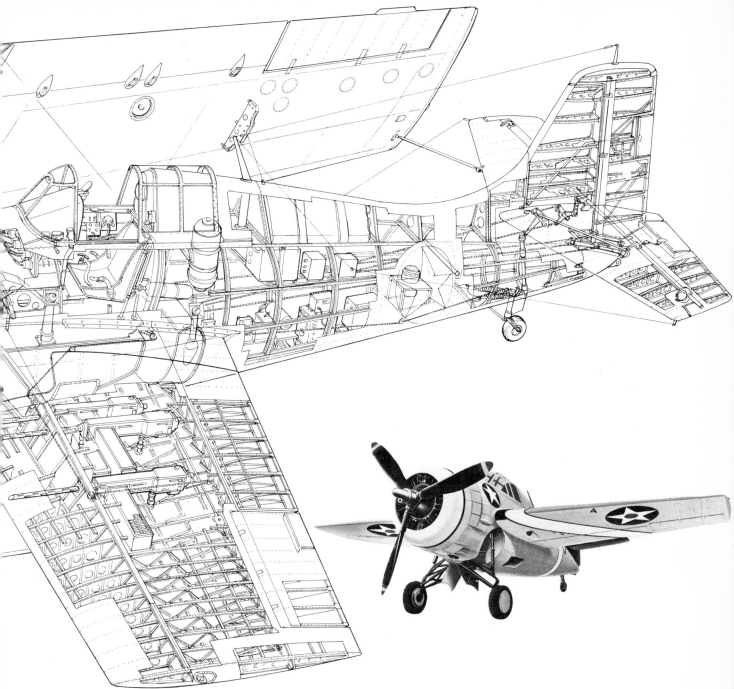

capabilities of overseas fighters such as the Bf 109 and Spitfire. U.S. aero engine manufacture was currently dominated by the impressive radials offered by Pratt & Whitney and Wright, so when Allison started to break into the American engine market-place from 1930 it decided to concentrate on the niche for powerful liquid-cooled engines. This stood the company in good stead when the 1937 specification was issued, its V-1710 being the only domestic inline engine suitable for the new fighters. The inline-engined derivative of the P-36 was the P-40 with the 1,150-hp (848-kW) V-1710-19, and this first flew in the autumn of 1938. The type was placed rapidly into production for the U.S. Army, and the type was widely delivered overseas as the Tomahawk and Kittyhawk. Though

Above: Based on the Beaufort torpedo bomber, the Bristol Beaufighter was first pressed into service as a night-fighter, but came into its own as a coastal and anti-shipping fighter carrying a torpedo or rockets.

schemed as a true fighter, the P-40 series in fact emerged as a decisive fighter-bomber, for its engine was fitted with a single-stage supercharger that resulted in a swift decline of power at medium altitudes. But at low altitudes the P-40 was fast, agile and viceless, and once fitted out with the full range of contemporary necessities (such as armour protection, self-sealing fuel tanks, etc) and bomb racks it emerged as an excellent low-level machine developed through many marks, and the P-40F and P-40L were variants fitted with the American-built version of the Merlin, the Packard V-1650-1, to run parallel with the Allison-engined models. Early marks were fitted with two synchronised 0.5-in and four unsynchronised 0.3-in machine-guns, while later models had six 0.5-in guns and provision for three 500-lb (227-kg) bombs.

The V-1710 inline engine was also employed by two other U.S. fighters of the period, the Lockheed P-38 Lightning and the Bell P-39 Airacobra. These were both unconventional fighters, the former being a twin-engined type with its tail mounted on long booms projecting from the rear of the engine nacelles, and the latter a single-engined type designed for high agility with its engine located on the centre of gravity and driving the propeller by means of a long extension shaft.

The P-38 originated from a 1936 requirement for a high-altitude interceptor, to which the fledgling Lockheed company (with

Left: Carrying a fixed armament of four 20-mm cannon and six 0.303-in (7.7-mm) machine-guns, the Beaufighter packed a devastating short-range punch to back up its longer-range weapons. These varied according to mark, the Beaufighter TF.Mk X having one 1,650- or 2,127-lb (748- or 965-kg) torpedo or eight 3-in (76-mm) unguided rockets.

Below: The Imperial Japanese Navy's most significant fighter in the opening stages of World War II was the Mitsubishi A6M Reisen (Zero Fighter), dubbed 'Zeke' by the Allies. This had good firepower, adequate performance, sparkling agility and phenomenal range. But the type lacked development potential and was soon obsolescent, though it remained in production throughout the war for lack of an adequate replacement.

previous experience only in high-performance light transports) responded with this extremely advanced concept. The core of the design was the engine installation, comprising a pair of V-1710 inlines whose nacelles were extended rearwards to provide the volume for the turbocharger and intercoolers demanded by each installation. This opened up the possibility of doing away with any conventional fuselage by extending the nacelles into true booms that supported the empennage. A central nacelle was all that was needed to accommodate the pilot, the extremely heavy armament of one 23-mm cannon and four 0.5-in machine-guns, and the nose unit of the radical nosewheel landing gear whose main units retracted into the booms.

The most interesting feature of the powerplant installation was the use of a turbocharger instead of a supercharger for each engine. The U.S.A. led the way with such power boosters, which are driven by exhaust gases rather than a mechanical output from the engine: the supercharger inevitably reduces the output available to the propeller, while the turbocharger uses the exhaust gases whose enormous dynamic potential is otherwise just spent into the outside air. There were considerable problems associated with the development of the turbocharger, which had to sustain the high temperature of the exhaust and turn at enormous speed as its compressors concentrated the indrawn air and passed it through coolers before it could be supplied to the engine. The problems were eventually solved, and the turbocharger installation became an integral part of most American aircraft designed for operation at high altitude. So sensitive were the Americans about the technology

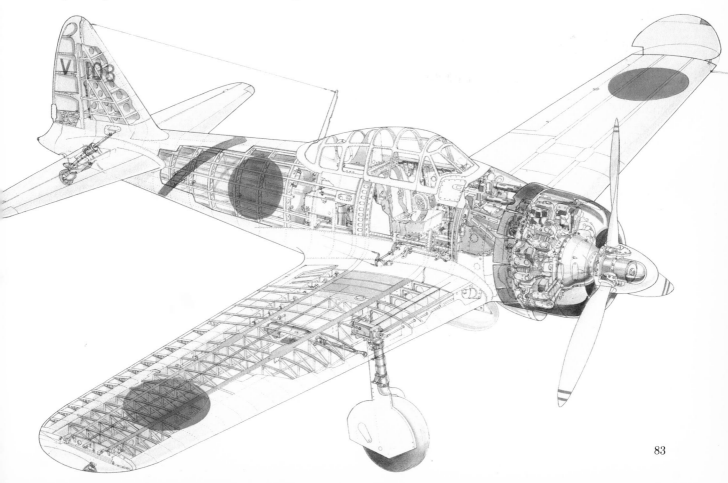

Left: The Fiat G.50 Freccia was an 'also ran' of World War II, lacking performance and firepower to a degree that could not be balanced by agility.

that they refused to allow the export of turbocharger-fitted aircraft to even their closest allies, reducing the performance of such aircraft to a drastic degree even when they were revised with a supercharger.

The first P-38 flew in January 1939, but the programme was still slow to deliver production aircraft and there were a large number of technical problems, both aerodynamic and mechanical, to be sorted out before small batches of P-38 and P-38D fighters could be delivered. They were in reality pre-production machines on which the operating service could come to grips with the new type. The Lightning was also being introduced as the lessons of intense air fighting over Europe were becoming available, and the results of these lessons were steadily incorporated before full-scale production could follow. The first genuine production model of the Lightning was therefore the P-38E, which began to enter service early in 1942. Thereafter the pace of development was rapid, and the Lightning matured as an exceptional warplane. It was rarely used in the interceptor role for which it had been designed, but proved itself as a long-range fighter and fighter-bomber (with an underwing armament of rockets and/or bombs) best suited to the requirements of the war against Japan. Here, in the vast reaches of the Pacific, the Lightning's range and twin-engined reliability were a profound advantage. The type was inevitably far less nimble than Japan's lightweight fighters, but it more than compensated for this in its extreme strength, high performance, devastating armament and the right tactics. In this last, the American pilots refused to be drawn into dogfights with the Japanese, instead operating at higher altitudes so that they could launch a diving attack, in which short bursts of heavy firepower tore apart the Japanese fighters, and then continue the high-speed dive to safety. The Lightning was the most successful Allied fighter of the war against Japan in terms of numbers of aircraft destroyed. The Lightning was also widely used for reconnaissance, the F-4 and F-5 variants usually containing a fan of five cameras in place of the nose armament.

Above: Another type that failed to make the grade as a fighter was the Bell Airacobra. This is a P-39D, basically similar to the P-39C initial-production model apart from having self-sealing fuel tanks, a feature proved essential from the earliest air combats of World War II.

The P-39 was no less unorthodox but in a totally different way. The type shared tricycle landing gear and a heavy nose armament with the P-38, but the P-39 was fitted with a 37-mm cannon in the nose, left free for this installation by the removal of the engine to a position just behind the pilot. The type first flew in 1939 and began to enter service in 1941, proving an immense disappointment: the Allison engine lost power rapidly at medium altitude, and the type's agility was decidedly inferior. On the other side of the coin, however, the P-39 was a capable gun platform and very strong: this commended the type to an alternative role in the fighter-bomber and close-support roles, where the pilot's good fields of vision and the heavy armament of one 37-mm cannon, two nose-mounted 0.5-in synchronised machine-guns and four wing-mounted 0.3-in unsynchronised machine-guns (revised in later models to one 37-mm and four 0.5-in guns) stood it in good stead. The Soviets received the bulk of Airacobra production. The P-63 Kingcobra was a developed model with greater power and laminar-flow wings, yet did no better as a fighter and was also used to good effect as a fighter-bomber.

The other new American fighters of the period were the U.S. Navy's first monoplane fighters, the portly and unsuccessful Brewster F2A Buffalo and the equally portly but redoubtable Grumman F4F Wildcat. Both used the same basic landing gear arrangement, with the main units designed to retract inward into the lower portion of the fuselage, and both were powered by the 1,200-hp (895-kW) Wright R-1820 Cyclone radial: the Buffalo was not a bad design, but lacked the edge or even any genuinely positive features that might have made it more effective; the Wildcat, on the other hand, proved a capable though limited fighter with great strength, good agility and an adequate battery of four 0.5-in guns. More importantly, perhaps, the Wildcat bridged the operational gap between the biplane fighters that preceded it and the fully-fledged successors such as the F6F Hellcat and Vought F4U Corsair. The Wildcat was also delivered in substantial numbers to the U.K., whose Royal Navy used the type with the name Martlet in replacement for unsuccessful two-seat types such as the Blackburn Roc and Skua, and mediocre types such as the Fairey Fulmar, again a two-seater. Like the land-based Boulton Paul Defiant, the Roc was produced to meet a requirement, ultimately proved to be totally inadequate for a two-seat fighter in which the armament was concentrated into a four-gun turret operated by the second crew member. Sized slightly larger than contemporary single-seaters, and powered by engines of about the same power, these turret fighters proved completely deficient in performance and agility: once the German fighter pilots had discovered their true disposition, they had an easy task to outmanoeuvre the turret fighters and shoot them down. The Defiant was ultimately pressed into service as an interim night-fighter, but soon passed into history, together with its tactical concept.

While the Americans had comparative leisure in which to develop their new fighters, on the other side of the Atlantic the pace of World War II was increasing and the demands on aircraft

Above: The Yakovlev Yak-3 was produced in parallel with the Yak-9, and was slightly smaller. Fitted with one 20-mm cannon and two 12.7-mm (0.5-in) guns, the Yak-3 was powered by a 1,220-hp (910-kW) Klimov M-105PF inline and topped 404 mph (650 km/h) at medium altitudes, but was generally used as escort for low-altitude attack aircraft such as the Ilyushin Il-2 and Petlyakov Pe-2.

Fw 190 V1 (prototype)

Fw 190A-4/R6

Fw 190A-6/R1

Fw 190A-0

Fw 190A-8/U1

Fw 190A-8 (Doppelreiter I)

Fw 190A-8 (SG116)

Fw 190C V18/U1

Fw 190D-9

Fw 190F-8

developing the whole time. In-service types were pushed through marks in rapid succession, and new types were urged through the development process as fast as possible. In the short term more importance was attached to the upgrading of current single-seaters, the Bf 109E giving way to the Bf 109F, the Hurricane Mk I to the Hurricane Mk II, and the Spitfire Mks I and II to the Spitfire Mk V. The Bf 109 had been planned as an offensive fighter within the context of air operations over the Blitzkrieg land campaign, and though this concept still retained a validity in the eyes of the German air force high command, the lessons of the Battle of Britain indicate that more emphasis should be placed on defensive fighters with a higher rate of climb and greater agility. The Bf 109F was thus powered by the 1,200-hp (895-kW) DB601N engine in a refined airframe of smoother line and fitted with revised wings and retractable tailwheel, the net effect being an increase in maximum speed from the 354 mph (570 km/h) of the Bf 109E to 382 mph (615 km/h) at rated altitude. The variant was also fitted with the GM-1 power-boost kit, allowing nitrous oxide to be fed into the engine for a considerable increase in short-term power. A retrograde step, however, was the downward revision of the armament to one 20-mm cannon and two 7.9-mm machine-guns, though the engine-mounted MG 151 cannon had a much faster rate of fire than the two wing-mounted MG FF cannon installed in the Bf 109E.

The Hurricane was now judged obsolescent in the light of first-line fighter capabilities and the increased flow of new Spitfires, but was upgraded into the Hurricane Mk II by the installation of the 1,460-hp (1,089-kW) Merlin XX with two-stage supercharger. This improved performance slightly, but the Hurricane was increasingly used as a low- and medium-altitude fighter-bomber in several subvariants: the Mk IIA was the last genuine fighter variant and had eight 0.303-in guns, while from the Mk IIB (12 0.303-in guns) the type was fitted with strengthened metal-skinned wings able to carry two 250- or 500-lb (113- or 227-kg) bombs; the Mk IIC had four 20-mm Hispano cannon, and the Mk IID featured two 40-mm cannon as a dedicated tank-killing aircraft.

Above: The Fw 190 was the best fighter deployed by Germany during World War II, and combined ease of production with excellent performance and firepower.

Below: The BMW 801C radial was used in the pre-production examples of the Focke-Wulf Fw 190.

Below: Cockpit of the FW 190A-8.

The Spitfire Mk V began to enter service in the spring of 1941, and was fitted with a variety of Merlin engines rated variously between 1,415 and 1,585 hp (1,056 and 1,182 kW) and optimised for low-, medium- and high-altitude work. The type was produced as the Mk VA with eight 0.303-in guns, the Mk VB with four 20-mm cannon, and the Mk VC with two 20-mm cannon and four 0.303-in guns, and this use of the A, B and C suffixes was retained to designate armament fits in later variants. The Spitfire Mk V proved highly successful in its first six months, but was then overtaken by the new Focke-Wulf Fw 190, whose advent in service came as a surprise and also as a rude shock to the British. Various expedients such as cropped wings and metal- rather than fabric-skinned ailerons were tried in an effort to provide the Spitfire Mk V with the same degree of low-level agility as the Fw 190A, but these were at best palliatives rather than solutions. A new mark was clearly needed, and when this began to appear the Mk V was increasingly relegated to the fighter-bomber role with provision for one 250- or 500-lb bomb carried under the fuselage.

Though the Bf 109 continued to enjoy widespread popularity, especially with the *Experten* (aces) who had grown up with it, the Fw 190 was by any objective standard Germany's finest and most versatile fighter of World War II, and as such one of the world's truly great aircraft. The type enjoyed a somewhat leisurely development as back-up to the Bf 109. The new fighter was designed by Kurt Tank, and throughout the design emphasis was placed on ease of production, sturdiness and the ability to accept change without complete disruption of the programme. The German authorities were initially loath to allow the use of a radial engine in the new fighter, but when the Fw 190 prototype first flew in June 1939 it was with a BMW 139 radial in a close-fitting cowl with ingenious air cooling arrangements. There were a number of teething problems as a result of the cooling, but the type soon began to mature as an excellent fighter characterised as a pilot's aeroplane: it had light yet well-balanced controls, wide-track inward-retracting landing gear and, perhaps most usefully for the combat

Right: Though based on the Wildcat, the Grumman F6F Hellcat was slightly larger and had considerably more power for superior performance and heavier armament. The type served from 1943 to 1945.

Left: The Ta 152 was the ultimate derivative of the Fw 190D series, with long-span wings for its role as a high-altitude interceptor.

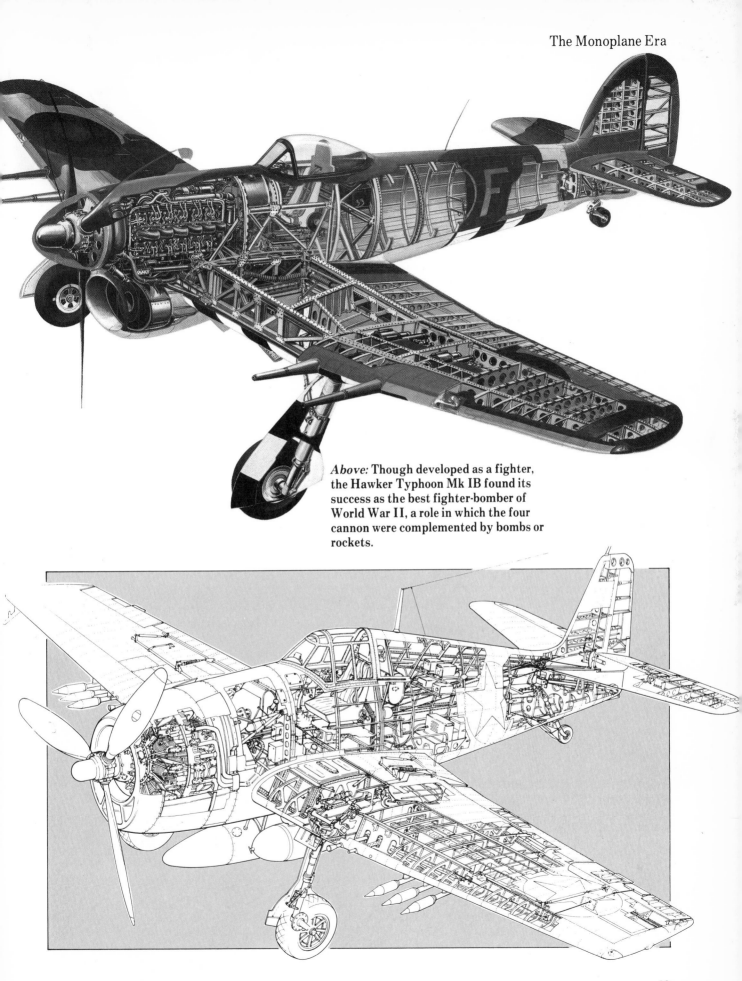

Above: Though developed as a fighter, the Hawker Typhoon Mk IB found its success as the best fighter-bomber of World War II, a role in which the four cannon were complemented by bombs or rockets.

Left: The P-51D was numerically and tactically the most important variant of the North American Mustang to see service in World War II. Fitted with a clear-vision canopy for all-round view, the P-51D was powered by the 1,490-hp (1,111-kW) Packard V-1650-7 and could attain 437 mph (703 km/h).

pilot, a *Kommandgerät* (control device) in which movement of the throttle automatically made for fuel flow correction, fuel mixture adjustment, propeller pitch setting and supercharger setting. The initial production model was the Fw 190A that began to enter service in September 1941, and this was powered by the 1,760-hp (1,313-kW) BMW 801 radial. Though this powerplant's output fell rapidly at height above 21,000 ft (6,400 m), below this height the Fw 190A was superior to the Spitfire Mk V in performance and agility in all aspects except tight turns. There was also a variant with

Below: Together with the Junkers Ju 88, the de Havilland Mosquito was the most versatile aircraft of World War II, serving with the utmost distinction in the bomber, night-fighter, heavy fighter and reconnaissance roles. The airframe was exceptionally clean, and its primary structure of balsa/plywood sandwich proved robust and easy to repair.

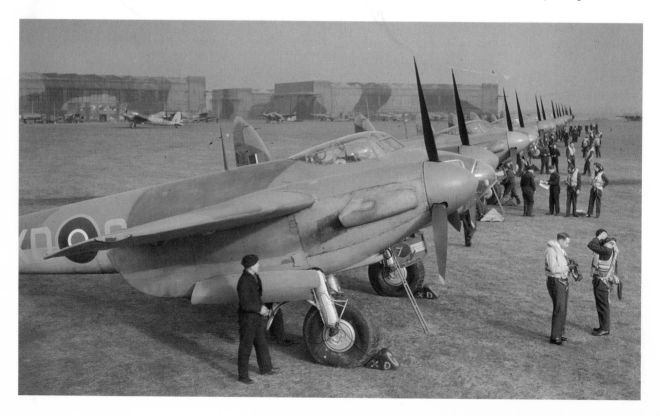

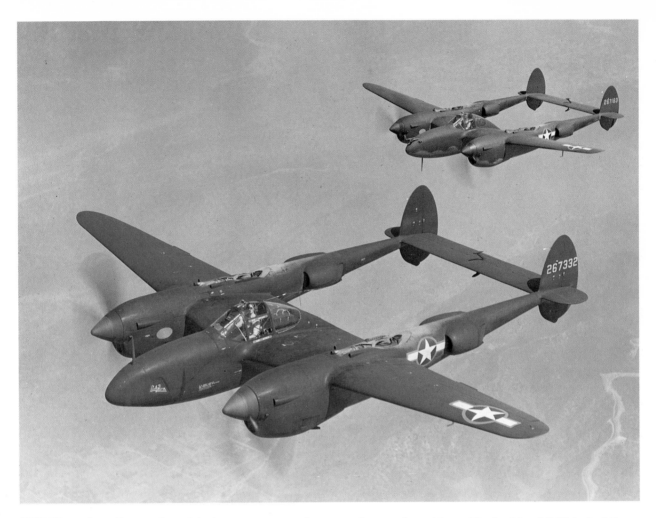

MW-50 methanol/water boost to increase power for a maximum of 10 minutes. The inbuilt armament was four 20-mm cannon (two fast-firing MG 151s and two slow-firing MG FFs) plus two 7.9-mm machine-guns, and from the beginning of its career the type was fitted as a fighter-bomber with capability for one 551-lb (250-kg) bomb. And it was as a low-level sneak raider with such a bombload that the Fw 190 first made its mark over southern England.

The Fw 190 was also well protected, the armour being well designed to shield the pilot and essential items from the most threatening aspects. The Fw 190 was produced in a bewildering number of variants and subvariants, the most important being the Fw 190D in which the radial engine was replaced by the 2,100-hp (1,567-kW) Junkers Jumo 213 inline, though this was fitted with an annular radiator that maintained the radial-engined appearance of the Fw 190. Even at the end of the war this was in every respect a formidable adversary, and was itself developed into the superb Ta 152 high-altitude fighter.

The British response to the Fw 190 was the Spitfire Mk IX, initially schemed as an interim measure pending the arrival of the definitive Spitfire Mk VIII (with a four-blade propeller driven by a Merlin 61 with a two-stage two-speed supercharger) but ultimately produced in larger numbers than any other Spitfire variant. The

Above: The Lockheed P-38 lacked the agility of single-engined fighters, but had excellent performance (especially in speed and range) and good firepower. These are an F-5B reconnaissance aircraft (foreground) derived from the P-38G, and a P-38J fighter.

Mk IX was powered by 1,655-hp (1,235-kW) Merlin 70 and offered the required increment of performance. Like the Mk V, the Mk IX was produced in low-, medium- and high-altitude versions, and though usually fitted with the C wing, it was also produced with the E wing mounting two 20-mm cannon and two 0.5-in machine-guns. The Spitfire Mk XVI was identical in all respects other than the powerplant, an American Packard-built Merlin 266. Further development of the Spitfire was centred on the use of the larger and more powerful Rolls-Royce Griffon engine, at first in the Spitfire Mk XII and then in the definitive Spitfire Mk XIV with teardrop hood and other improvements. The Spitfire was also developed as an excellent high-altitude photo-reconnaissance aircraft, and as the Seafire naval fighter. The ultimate developments of the series were the post-war Spiteful land and Seafang naval fighters, which were produced in only very small numbers and were amongst the world's fastest piston-engined aircraft.

By this time the U.S.A. was firmly embroiled in World War II and, in addition to the land-based fighters mentioned above, was beginning to introduce two other land-based machines. In totally different ways these were complementary classics: the Republic

Above: The Junkers Ju 88G-6 was a dedicated night-fighter variant of a design originally evolved as a high-speed bomber. Performance was inevitably degraded by the drag-inducing antenna array on the nose, yet the Ju 88G-6 had a respectable turn of speed, topping 345 mph (555 km/h) at altitude, and carried the formidable armament of four fixed forward-firing 20-mm MG 151.20 cannon, two similar cannon in a fixed dorsal installation to fire obliquely upwards and forward in the belly over bombers overhead, and a defensive 13-mm (0.51-in) MG 151 machine-gun.

Left: The Yakovlev Yak-9D was the variant of the family optimised for bomber escort duties with extra fuel at the expense of armament. Range was a useful 870 miles (1,400 km), increased in the Yak-9DD derivative to 1,367 miles (2,200 km).

Below: The Lavochkin La-7 was a classic medium-altitude fighter, developed from the La-5 by careful aerodynamic refinement and reduced fuel capacity to provide usefully improved performance with the same basic powerplant, the Shvetsov ASh-82 radial, and armament increased from two to three 20-mm ShVAK cannon.

P-47 Thunderbolt was a huge fighter known as the 'Jug', and the North American P-51 Mustang was a comparative lightweight of angular grace and extraordinary performance. The P-47 was schemed round a Pratt & Whitney R-2800 Double Wasp with its associated turbocharger in the rear fuselage, where it was fed by exhaust gases channelled from the engine in an asbestos-lined pipe to compress air that had to make a 43-ft (13.1-m) return trip from the nose-mounted inlet via the turbocharger and back to the engine. This all required a massive fuselage supported by substantial wings that allowed the devastating armament of eight 0.5-in machine-guns. The P-47B began to enter service in the spring of 1943, the P-47C introduced a ventral tank to boost fuel capacity, and the most prolific model was the P-47D and almost identical P-47G (12,956 built) with a teardrop canopy, provision for 2,500 lb (1,134 kg) of bombs or 10 rockets, and water-boosting for a maximum speed of 433 mph (607 km/h). The two ultimate variants were the P-47M with short-range 'sprint' performance, and the P-47N long-range model for Pacific operations.

Right: The F4U-1 was the first production version of the mighty Vought Corsair fighter, introduced in 1943 with a 2,000-hp (1,492-kW) Pratt & Whitney R-2800 Double Wasp radial and an armament of six 0.5-in (12.7-mm) machine-guns.

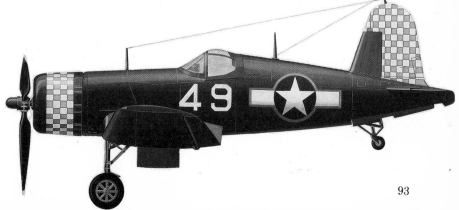

Below: But for official resistance to its Bristol Centaurus radial, the Hawker Tempest Mk II could have emerged as a great combat fighter.

The P-51 was spurred by a British requirement of 1940, and developed in the remarkably short period of 117 days to an initial flight in October 1940. Great emphasis was placed on low drag (through careful fuselage design and a laminar-flow wing) to ensure high performance and long range, and the design was optimised for ease of production and great first-line reliability. The result was probably the greatest fighter of World War II, a design that seemed to possess boundless development 'stretch' without adverse effect on handling, and the ability to handle just about every task considered for it. The original model had a 1,150-hp (848-kW) Allison V-1710 engine and various armament fits centred on six or eight 0.5- and 0.3-in machine-guns. The Allison used in this initial model suffered the basic failing of all V-1710 engines, and performed with great indifference at all but low altitudes. The initial Mustangs were thus used for tactical reconnaissance and close support, proving themselves capable machines with the ability to carry two 500-lb bombs. The U.S. Army adopted the specialised designation A-36 to cover these low-level attack aircraft. The Mustang was made by the decision to recast the design with a Packard-built Merlin engine in the P-51B and P-51C, which entered service at the end of 1943 with totally improved performance and a standard armament of four 0.5-in guns. Range was excellent, and with an escort of such fighters the heavy bombers of the U.S.A.A.F. could at last probe deep into Germany without the catastrophic losses that had hitherto resulted from such efforts. Further development produced the definitive P-51D (7,956 built) with a cut-down rear fuselage, teardrop canopy, six-gun armament with provision for 2,000 lb (907 kg) of bombs or 10 5-in (127-mm) rockets and the 1,790-hp (1,335-kW) V-1610-7 Merlin for a maximum speed of 443 mph (713 km/h) and a range of 2,080 miles

Above right: The most far-sighted fighter of World War II was the Messerschmitt Me 262 fighter, an elegant and hard-hitting fighter delayed for political reasons and then hampered by the chronic unreliability of its axial-flow turbojet engines.

Left: The only inline-engined fighter to serve the Imperial Japanese forces in quantity, and dubbed 'Tony' by the Allies, the Kawasaki Ki-61 Hien was an effective fighter with adequate armament, but lacked the development potential to match newer Allied fighters as the war progressed.

Below: The Dornier Do 335 was a fascinating attempt to produce a heavy fighter with twin 1,900-hp (1,417-kW) DB 603 inlines located in nose and tail for higher performance and minimal single-engine asymmetry problems.

(3,347 km) with internal and external fuel. In a fascinating expansion of the concept, a twin-engined variant was produced as the P-82 Twin Mustang by marrying two P-51s and their outer wing panels with a common parallel-chord centre section and tailplane for yet longer range and two pilots to reduce fatigue in long flights.

With the exception of U.S.A.A.F. units in the South-West Pacific and China, the brunt of the air war against Japan was borne by the U.S. Navy and U.S. Marine Corps. Their principal fighter was initially the F4F Wildcat, but from 1943 this was rapidly supplanted by the Grumman F6F Hellcat, which retained the same basic design philosophy as its predecessor but was fitted with the 2,000-hp (1,492-kw) R-2800 Double Wasp. The type was slightly larger than the Wildcat, and the prototype first flew in June 1942. Performance was adequate given the generally low performance of the opposing

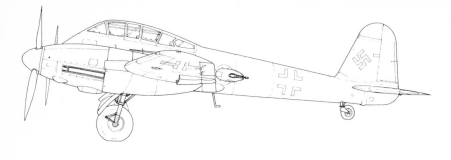

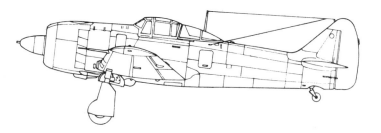

Left: The Kawasaki Ki-100 was the Ki-61
reworked to accept the 1,500-hp
(1,119-kW) Mitsubishi Ha.112 radial, and
proved a useful (though again limited)
fighter.

Japanese fighters, but the keynotes of the design were structural strength combined with hard-hitting firepower in the form of six 0.5-in guns. Some 12,270 Hellcats were built, and the type served with great distinction in the hands of the U.S. Navy and Royal Navy. It was later adapted as a fighter-bomber with two 1,000-lb bombs or rockets. There was also a night-fighter version with radar. The ultimate product of this design effort was the Grumman F8F Bearcat, which was too late for World War II but served for a short time thereafter pending the delivery of jet-powered fighters. In this machine the R-2800 engine was retained in an airframe cut down in weight as well as size, and refined aerodynamically in comparison with that of the F6F for superior climb performance and ceiling with an armament of four 0.5-in guns, later revised to a quartet of 20-mm cannon.

The Vought F4U Corsair was in fact earlier in origin than the Hellcat, having first flown in May 1940. The type was conceptually

Below: British naval fighters were generally hampered by the official demand for a two-man crew, yet the Fairey Firefly Mk I performed moderately well on its 1,730-hp (1,290-kW) Rolls-Royce Griffon IIB and packed a considerable punch with its four 20-mm cannon plus two 1,000-lb (454-kg) bombs or eight 60-lb (27-kg) rockets.

96

Right: The Kawanishi N1K2-J Shiden (violet lightning) was dubbed 'George' by the Allies, and was one of the best Japanese fighters of World War II. The type was evolved from the N1K1 'Rex' floatplane fighter as a land-based machine with the 1,990-hp (1,484-kW) Nakajima Homare 21 radial, a maximum speed of 370 mph (595 km/h) and an armament of four 20-mm cannon.

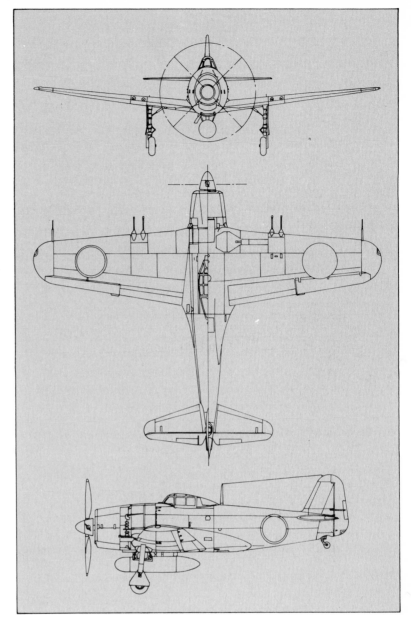

Above: The N1K2-J was comparatively easy to build, and like most Japanese fighters was characterised by a high rate of climb and great agility.

very advanced, with inverted gull wings so that the length of the landing gear legs could be kept as short as possible and the folded height of the wings reduced to a minimum. The design suffered from a diversity of teething problems, and began to enter service only late in 1942. The U.S. Navy distrusted the type's comparatively high landing speed, and the Corsair matured as a truly formidable warplane with excellent performance and the potent warload of six 0.5-in guns or four 20-mm cannon plus two 1,000-lb bombs or eight rockets. Power was provided by an R-2800 Double Wasp, providing this doubty performer with the capability to undertake roles as diverse as night-fighting, close support and interception. Like the P-51 Mustang, the Corsair went on to expand its reputation and capabilities in the post-war world.

Numerically the most significant fighters faced by the Americans in the Pacific were the Imperial army's Nakajima Ki-43 Hayabusa

(peregrine falcon), dubbed 'Oscar' by the Allies, and the Imperial navy's Mitsubishi A6M Zero Fighter, dubbed 'Zeke' by the Allies. These were successors to the Ki-27 and A5M respectively, continuing in the Japanese philosophy of lightweight fighters of great agility. The Ki-43 was an elegant low-wing monoplane with retractable landing gear, and performed creditably on the 1,000 hp of its Nakajima Ha-25 radial, which was replaced by more powerful Nakajima radials in successive models. The type first flew in 1939 and began to enter service late in 1941, but was drastically undergunned with a pair of 7.7- or later 12.7-mm machine-guns, and lacked the structural strength and performance to match the later American fighters.

Above: One Hawker Tempest Mk II was reworked as a prototype Fury with Griffon 85 inline and contra-rotating propellers, but development of the Tempest's concept led ultimately to the magnificent Sea Fury (below) with the Bristol Centaurus radial.

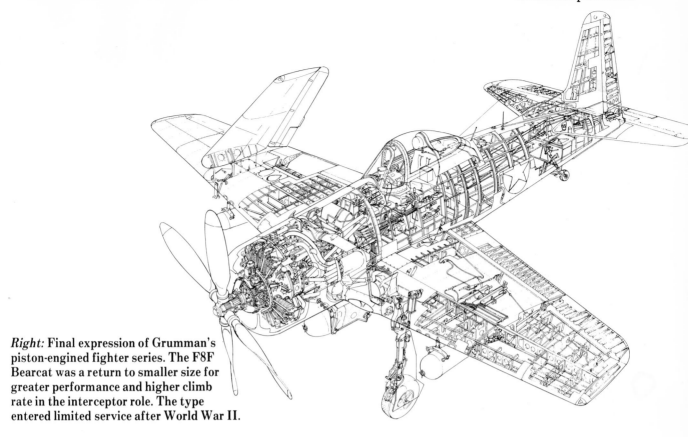

Right: Final expression of Grumman's piston-engined fighter series. The F8F Bearcat was a return to smaller size for greater performance and higher climb rate in the interceptor role. The type entered limited service after World War II.

Much the same can be said of the A6M, which was undoubtedly the finest naval fighter in the world at the time of its introduction late in 1940. Like other Japanese fighters the 'Zeke' was formidably agile. At the time of its debut it was well-armed with two 20-mm cannon and two 7.7-mm machine-guns, and also possessed good performance in all regimes thanks to its 950-hp (709-kW) Nakajima Sakae radial. Perhaps the A6M's greatest attribute, however, was its prodigious range through provision of extensive internal and external tankage combined with light structure weight and special training in flying the fighter with the engine running at the leanest of lean mixtures. This allowed the Japanese to operate over parts of the Pacific though inaccessible to them, giving them a powerful tactical edge in the period of their expansion. But then the A6M's light weight began to tell against it as the larger, faster and more powerful American fighters began to appear: power was increased and armament bolstered, but the Zero Fighter could not be brought up to the level of the American fighters in strength and protection. The Japanese made strenuous efforts later in the war to produce fighters adequate to the tasks of matching the American fighters and dealing with the American strategic bombers, but could produce these new types (typically the Kawasaki N1K 'George' and Ki-45 'Randy', the Mitsubishi J2M 'Jack', and the Nakajima Ki-44 'Tojo' and Ki-84 'Frank') in only small numbers. The sole exception was the Kawasaki Ki-61 Hien (swallow), dubbed 'Tony' by the Allies, which was the only Japanese inline-engined fighter to be used in large numbers. Powered by the 1,175-hp (877-kW) Kawasaki Ha. 40, the Ki-61 had adequate performance but only modest armament in

Below: The Messerschmitt Me 163 was a rocket-powered point-defence interceptor as dangerous to its pilots as to its enemies. The type landed on a skid.

Bottom: The Me 263 was developed from the Me 163 with greater range and retractable wheeled landing gear. It never became operational.

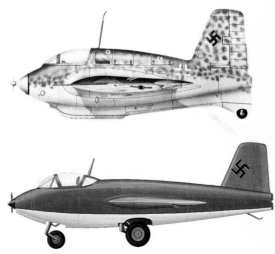

the form of two 20-mm cannon and two 12.6-mm machine-guns.

A similar tendency was afflicting the Italians, who had started World War II with the same basic attitude as the Japanese and began to pay the penalty from 1941 as they encountered later Allied fighters. Though limited by their lack of suitable engines and effective firepower, the Italian fighters were in themselves potentially excellent. Thus the use of German engines and armament allowed a radical transformation of capability that was then let down only by Italy's inadequate manufacturing base. The G.50 Freccia was revised as the G.55 Centauro with a licence-built version of the Daimler-Benz DB 605A inline and a cannon armament to become a first-class fighter; the C.200 Saetta was upgunned slightly and given a licence-built DB 601A to become the useful C.202 Folgore, and then transformed yet again to become the powerful C.205 Veltro with a licence-built DB 605A and cannon armament; and the Re.2000 was improved into the Re.2001 with a DB 601A and slightly heavier machine-gun armament, and then into the Re.2005 with a DB 605A and cannon armament.

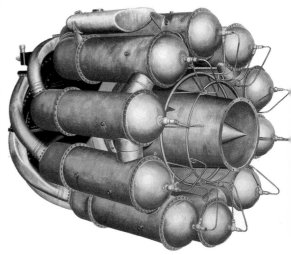

The same DB 605A was used to transform the Bf 109F into the Bf 109G, which was produced in large numbers and in a multitude of subvariants in Germany's desperate effort to find a counter to the increasing numbers of high-quality fighters fielded by both the Western Allies and the Soviets. The 'Gustav' was introduced late in 1942, and while the new powerplant did succeed in boosting performance, this was achieved only at the expense of handling. Moreover, the need to upgrade the armament resulted in extra weight and bulges over the engine cowling to accommodate the breeches of the 13.1-mm (0.52-in) machine-guns carried over the engine to supplement the 20-mm (or in later variants 30-mm) cannon firing through the propeller hub. The Bf 109K was essentially similar to the Bf 109G.

The threat faced by the German air units on the Eastern Front had grown enormously between 1941 and 1943. At the time of Germany's invasion of the U.S.S.R. in July 1941 the Soviets had been equipped with obsolete or obsolescent fighters such as the Polikarpov I-15 biplane and I-16 monoplane, albeit in their late-production forms with useful armament but inadequate performance. However, a massive effort had then transformed the situation, and by the time of Germany's decisive defeat in the Battle

Top: The Gloster Meteor was the world's first jet fighter to become operational, and though of only limited capability and development potential, served the U.K. faithfully in a number of roles for many years.

Above: The Whittle turbojet was produced in the face of official indifference until it began to show its true potential, but then the initial dedicated effort was scattered by ministry insistence that all manner of industrial concerns should become involved in the programme.

Right: The Messerschmitt Me 210 was a first attempt towards the evolution of a heavy fighter more successful than the Bf 110, but was plagued by aerodynamic problems and succeeded rapidly by the Me 410.

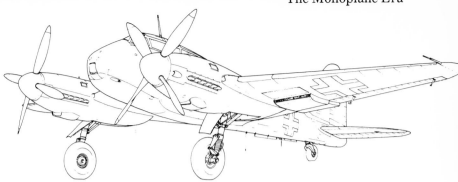

of Kursk during July 1943 the Soviets were fielding superb types such as the Lavochkin La-5 with the 1,640-hp (1,223-kW) Shvetsov ASh-82 radial and two 20-mm cannon, and the Yakovlev Yak-9 with the 1,260-hp (940-kW) Klimov M-105 inline and a wide assortment of cannon/machine-gun armament in a large number of variants. These were partnered by declining quantities of older types such as the LaGG-3, Yak-3 and Yak-7, which were still moderately effective but concentrated mainly on the ground-attack role. These fighters were not as advanced technically as their German opponents, but were powerfully armed, immensely sturdy, admirably suited to the exigencies of operations on the Eastern Front, available in large numbers and, just as importantly, flown by pilots who were now beginning to show skills comparable to those of the German pilots.

At this time the British were making very successful use of the Hawker Typhoon, which had been conceived before the war by Camm as a fighter successor to the Hurricane with the 2,200-hp (1,641-kW) Napier Sabre inline and an armament of 12 0.303-in machine-guns (Typhoon Mk IA) or four 20-mm cannon (Typhoon Mk IIB). The prototype flew in February 1940, and the type began to enter service in mid-1941. The Typhoon proved unsuccessful as a fighter, but was developed as an exceptional fighter-bomber with the cannon armament and either two 1,000-lb bombs or eight 3-in

Below: The Brewster Buffalo was the U.S. Navy's first monoplane fighter, but was essentially an interim type that lacked the performance for effective first-line use. The type was used operationally as a landplane by the Finns against the Soviets, and by the British against the Japanese.

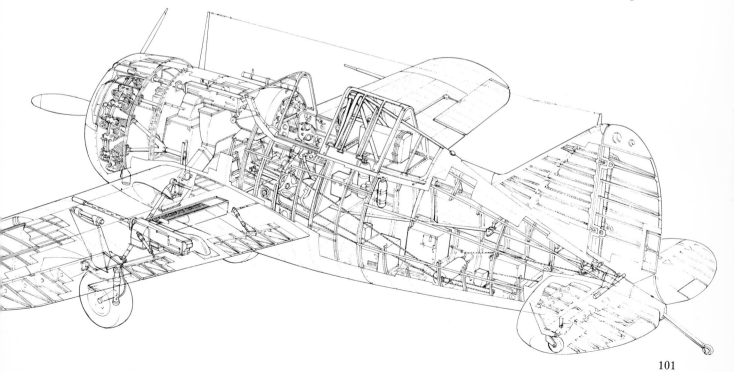

(76-mm) rockets. But Camm had already moved on to a 'Typhoon II' concept with a teardrop canopy, a thinner wing and an improved Sabre with four- rather than three-blade propeller. This was the Tempest, which first flew in February 1943. Prototypes were evaluated with three different engines, and production contracts were placed for the Tempest Mk II with the Bristol Centaurus radial and the Tempest Mk V with the Sabre. The latter entered service in useful numbers, and proved itself an admirable fighter and fighter-bomber. The Tempest Mk II was too late for World War II, but was produced in small numbers for post-war service, and also paved the way for the Sea Fury, the finest piston-engined fighter ever produced.

World War II also saw the emergence of the night-fighter as a weapon in its own right, and here twin-engined aircraft predominated. Such fighters had earlier been envisaged in the daylight bomber-destroyer role with a two/three-man crew and heavy cannon armament: typical of the overall concept was the Messerschmitt Bf 110 of 1939, which in its Bf 110C variant was powered by a 1,100-hp (821-kW) DB 601A inlines and fitted with a nose armament of two 20-mm cannon plus four 7.9-mm machine-guns, vestigial rearward defence being provided by a trainable 7.9-mm gun. Combat experience in 1940 had shown the severe performance and agility limitations of the type, especially against single-seat fighters, and it was only when these heavy twin-engined machines were developed as radar-equipped night-fighters that they really came into their own. The definitive night-fighter version of

Above: The Yakovlev Yak-15 was a radical reworking of the Yak-3 piston-engined fighter with an RD-10 turbojet in the nose of the pod-and-boom fuselage as an interim jet fighter immediately after World War II.

Below: The Kyushu J7W Shinden (magnificent lightning) was a prototype of exceptional promise, a canard pusher design offering exceptional performance with heavy nose-mounted armament.

the Bf 110G series was equipped with two 1,425-hp (1,063-kW) DB 605B engines and an armament of two 30-mm and two 20-mm fixed cannon plus two trainable 7.9-mm machine-guns. Other twin-engined night-fighters were the Heinkel He 219, and specialized version of the Dornier Do 217 and Junkers Ju 88 high-speed bombers. The Germans also developed the Messerschmitt Me 210 and Me 410 twin-engined tactical fighters.

The British night-fighting role got under way with the Bristol Beaufighter, which found more successful employment as a coastal anti-shipping fighter, but the main British night-fighter was the superlative de Havilland Mosquito, which was built largely of balsa/plywood sandwich and powered by twin Merlin engines. This most versatile of World War II aircraft was equally at home in the light bombing, (anti-ship) fighter-bombing, night-fighting and photo-reconnaissance roles. The night-fighter series started with the interim NF.Mk II, but soon evolved into the more capable

Above: The Heinkel He 219A Uhu (owl) was Germany's best night-fighter of World War II, powered by two 1,900-hp (1,417-kW) DB 603G inlines and featuring the prodigious armament of six 30-mm and two 20-mm cannon. Procurement was severely hampered by political opposition.

Below: The Heinkel He 162A Salamander was designed as a *Volksjäger* (people's fighter) with good performance and adequate firepower in an airframe designed for simple manufacture in enormous quantities for operation by pilots of very limited flight experience.

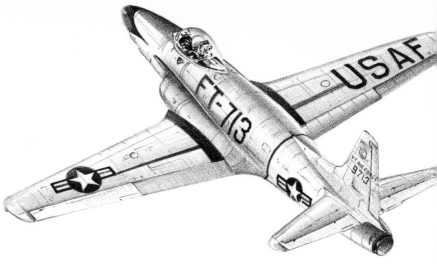

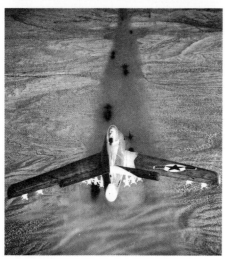

Top: The Lockheed P-80 Shooting Star was an excellent fighter for its period, but was just too late for World War II.

Above right: The P-80B second production model was very similar to the P-80A apart from an uprated engine and thinner wing.

Above and above right: Republic designed its F-84 as the Thunderjet with a straight wing, but when the lessons of German and then American research into swept wings had been digested the type (by then redesignated F-84) was recast with swept wings as the F-84F Thunderstreak, which was used mainly for reconnaissance and long-range strike.

NF.Mk XII and similar NF.Mk XVII with American radar, the longer-ranged NF.Mk XIII and similar NF.Mk XIX with American radar, and the definitive NF.Mk 30. This last was powered by 1,710-hp (1,276-kW) Merlin 72s and could attain 397 mph (639 km/h) with an armament of four 20-mm cannon. From the same basic concept as the Mosquito sprang the finest twin-engined fighter ever developed, the de Havilland Hornet long-range single-seater with a pair of 2,030-hp (1,514-kW) Merlin 130/131s for a maximum speed of 451 mph (726 km/h) over a range of 2,500 miles (4,023 km) with an armament of four 20-mm cannon and up to 2,000 lb of disposable stores. The Hornet was too late for service in World War II, but served in small numbers after the war and provided the basis for the Sea Hornet naval version.

American forces had a more limited requirement for night-fighters, and after the interim Douglas A-20 Havoc bomber conversion and a number of modified single-seaters, the primary type was the Northrop P-61 Black Widow, a monumental design with two R-2800 Double Wasp radials, a maximum speed of 362 mph (583 km/h) and an armament of four 20-mm fixed cannon and four 0.5-in machine-guns in a trainable upper-fuselage barbette.

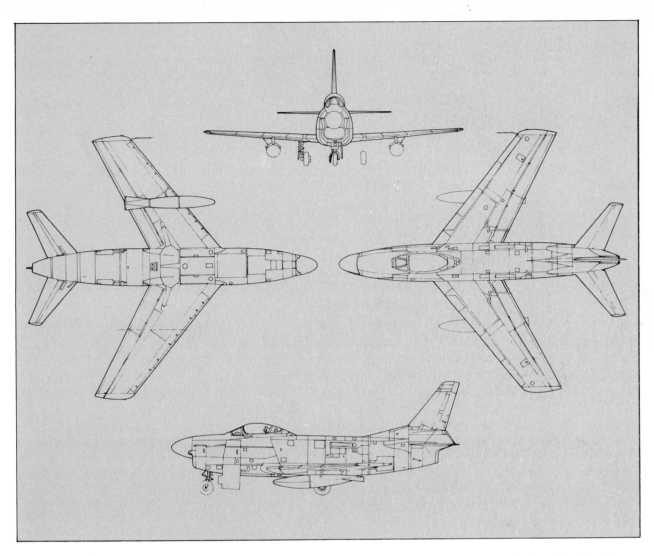

World War II also saw the emergence of the turbojet-powered fighter, although only on a limited scale. The two types to enter service were one British and one German type, the former being the Gloster Meteor and the latter the Messerschmitt Me 262. The Meteor was an entirely conventional fighter by the standards of its day in all but its powerplant, which comprised two massive centrifugal-flow turbojets in wing-mounted nacelles. The first prototype flew in March 1943, and the type was evaluated with different engines until the 1,700-lb (771-kg) thrust Rolls-Royce Welland I was selected for the Meteor F.Mk I, which began to enter service in July 1944. The Meteor was soon involved in the defence against the V-1 flying bomb: the Meteor was one of the few fighters fast enough to catch this in level flight at low altitude. The F.Mk I was soon joined by the Meteor F.Mk III with 2,000-lb (907-kg) thrust Derwent I turbojets, and the armament of both variants was the standard quadruple fit of 20-mm cannon in the forward fuselage. The Meteor was little more than the current concept for a piston-engined fighter modified for jet engines, but nevertheless went on to a successful post-war career as a fighter, and later as a night-fighter and trainer in a succession of upengined marks. The Meteor was

Above: **The North American F-86D Sabre was a definitive model of this first swept-wing American fighter, carrying nose radar for all-weather interception capability.**

Left: The Lavochkin La-9 was the ultimate development of this design bureau's experience with piston-engined fighters, and was powered by the Shvetsov ASh-82FNV radial for a maximum speed of 429 mph (690 km/h).

supplemented immediately after the war by the de Havilland Vampire, a beautiful and diminutive machine of remarkably good performance with a single de Havilland Goblin turbojet (fed through lateral inlets) in the central nacelle aft of the pilot and four-cannon armament: the empennage was supported on slender booms projecting from the unswept wing.

The Me 262 was a more advanced concept with a pair of 1,984-lb (900-lb) thrust Junkers Jumo 004B axial-flow turbojets in slim nacelles slung under the modestly swept wings. By mid-1942 the Me 262 was proving itself an exceptional type, but the German authorities saw no virtue in an expensive development programme that would yield fruit only after Germany had won the way with its current generation of piston-engined fighters. Thus it was November 1943 before production was authorised – and then only on Hitler's express condition that the type be used as a fast bomber

Below: Produced by de Havilland as a lightweight interceptor, the Vampire was just too late for World War II, but served ably in the next years as a fighter, fighter-bomber and trainer. The large diameter of the central nacelle was dictated by the fact that the de Havilland Ghost engine was of the centrifugal-flow type.

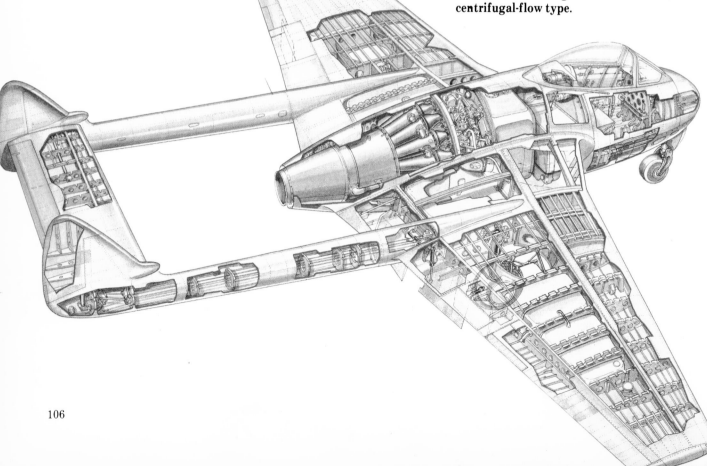

Above: The Dornier Do 335 was too late for World War II, and the development of heavy piston-engined fighters of this type was not pursued as the jet engine clearly offered far greater development potential.

with two 500-kg (1,102-lb) bombs. The Me 262 finally became operational in September 1944, but many precious months had been wasted and this great fighter was thereafter beset by constant retreat and fuel shortages so that it had only a limited chance to use its four 30-mm nose cannon in anger. Another German jet fighter that saw limited use was the Heinkel He 162, which featured a 1,764-lb (800-kg) thrust BMW 003E turbojet in a nacelle above the rear fuselage.

The U.S.A.'s first jet fighter was the Bell P-59 Airacomet, but this was a failure. The next type was the Lockheed P-80 Shooting Star, but this was just too late for service in World War II. The type entered extensive service after the war as the F-80, however: it was powered in its F-80A form by a 4,000-lb (1,814-kg) General Electric J33 axial-flow turbojet, and led to the T-33 trainer still in

Below: The Hawker Sea Hawk was designed as a first-generation naval fighter of the jet-powered variety, and was soon overtaken in the pure fighter role by more capable types, thereafter being developed for ground-attack work in forms such as this Sea Hawk FGA.Mk 4 with four inbuilt 20-mm cannon and underwing loads such as four 500-lb (227-kg) bombs or 20 3-in (76-mm) rockets with 60-lb (27-kg) warheads.

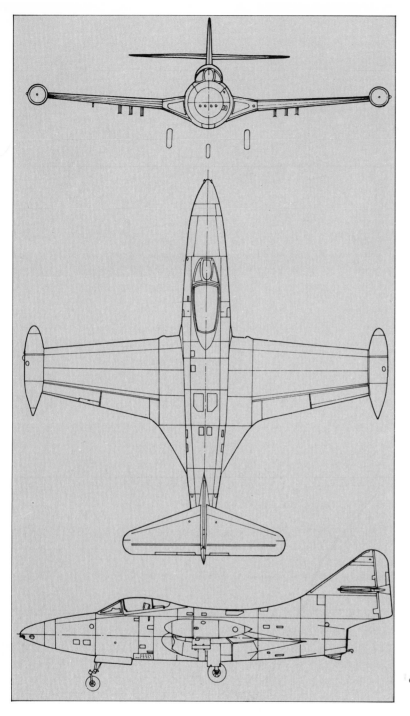

Left: The Grumman F9F Panther is a good example of the evolution of fighter design in the late 1940s. The type was designed in 1945 with a quartet of Westinghouse J30 turbojets buried in the wings, but then revised to accommodate a single 5,000-lb (2,272-kg) thrust Pratt & Whitney J42, as the Rolls-Royce Nene was designated for U.S. manufacture. The design was revised in later marks for the more powerful Pratt & Whitney J48, an engine type carried over into the F9F Cougar series with swept rather than straight wings. The armament was four 20-mm cannon and various underwing loads.

widespread service, and also to the F-94 Starfire two-seat all-weather fighter with an afterburning Pratt & Whitney J48 engine and, in the radar-equipped F-94C variant, an armament of 48 unguided rockets in the nose and two wingtip pods.

There were many other jet fighters in the period immediately after World War II, but again these epitomised little more than the piston-engined philosophy translated into turbojet power. The real change came with the emergence of two new fighters from the newly-emerged superpowers: the Mikoyan-Gurevich MiG-15 in the U.S.S.R. and the North American F-86 Sabre in the U.S.A.

Below: The Saab J 29 was Sweden's second jet fighter. Coming as it did after the interim Saab J 21R, it was a thoroughly workmanlike design well up to the standards of its day.

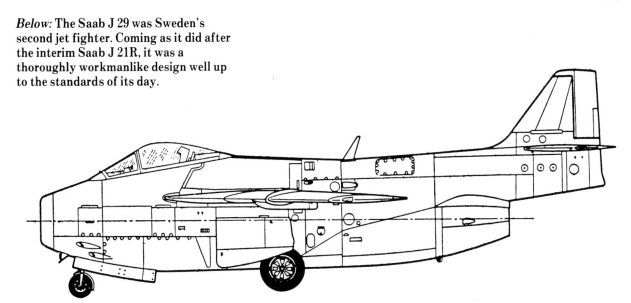

Below: The U.S.S.R.'s first fully-fledged jet fighter was the MiG-15, the F-86 Sabre's main opponent in the Korean War and still widely used by smaller countries for advanced and conversion training.

1954-1965
The Jet Fighter Comes of Age

Appearing on opposite sides of the Iron Curtain at about the same time, the Mikoyan-Gurevich MiG-15 and North American F-86 Sabre make an interesting contrast in their respective national design philosophies and capabilities, especially as both these fighters drew heavily on the corpus of German experimental data captured by the Soviets and Americans in the closing stages of World War II.

The Soviets' efforts to produce a jet-powered fighter had already started with indigenous research during World War II, but were hastily revised to make maximum use of captured German data and engines, the latter being more advanced than the current Soviet equivalents. These efforts bore fruit with interim fighters designed round a pod-and-boom concept: the powerplant was located in the forward part of the fuselage (the pod) together with its circular inlet, the pilot and the armament, exhausting through a simple nozzle or nozzles at the rear of the pod under the boom that supported the tail unit. Typical of these straight-winged fighters were the Mikoyan-Gurevich MiG-9 and two 1,764-lb (800-kg) thrust RD-20 turbojets, as the Soviets designated their development of the BMW 003, and the Yakovlev Yak-15 with one 1,984-lb (900-kg) thrust RD-10 turbojet, as the Soviets designated their development of the Junkers Jumo 004. The Yak-17 was then revised as the Yak-17 with tricycle rather than tailwheel landing gear, and the concept was then applied to the new Yak-23 powered by a 3,527-lb (1,600-kg) thrust RD-500, as the Soviets designated their Rolls-Royce Derwent development. These fighters offered modest improvements in performance over current piston-engined types, and thus served a useful tactical function, but more significantly allowed the Soviets to move at minimum risk into the jet fighter business, whose first genuinely Soviet result was the MiG-15, dubbed 'Fagot' by NATO.

By any standards the MiG-15 was an enormous achievement: the type was powered by the Soviet derivative of the Rolls-Royce Nene (the Klimov-engineered RD-45), and featured a tubby fuselage (required for the large-diameter of the centrifugal-flow engine), tricycle landing gear, an advanced wing swept at 35°, and a massive vertical tail that was highly swept to increase the moment of the tailplane located two-thirds of the way up it. This latter allowed a comparatively short (and thus effective) jetpipe together with adequate longitudinal control. The programme for the MiG-15 was authorised in March 1946, the first prototype flew in 1947, and the type began to enter service at the end of 1948. The performance contrast with earlier fighters was enormous: with 5,015-lb (2,275-kg)

thrust available from its RD-45F turbojet, the MiG-15 attained 652.5 mph (1,050 km/h) at sea level (equivalent to Mach 0.86), climbed to 32,810 ft (10,000 m) in 7 minutes 5 seconds, and possessed a service ceiling of 49,870 ft (15,200 m). The armament comprised one 37-mm and two 23-mm cannon. Extensive trials were carried out with the MiG-15, and these soon led to the improved MiG-15bis with an all-flying, or slab, tailplane for better longitudinal control at high Mach, whose compressibility problems were only just being explored. The MiG-15bis was introduced in 1950 with the 5,952-lb (2,700-kg) thrust Klimov VK-1, a development of the RD-45, and improved performance, including a climb to 32,810 ft in 5 minutes 30 seconds and a service ceiling of 50,855 ft (15,500 m).

The Americans had meanwhile been working their way along a similar course, the interim straight-winged fighters being types such as the land-based F-80 already mentioned and the Republic F-84 Thunderjet, plus the carrierborne McDonnell FH-1 Phantom, McDonnell F2H Banshee and Grumman F9F Panther. It is worth noting, however, that two of these types were later revised with swept wings to maintain their currency as first-line fighters, the results being the F-84F Thunderstreak fighter-bomber and the

Above: The Dassault Mystère IVA was a fine example of the first generation of swept-wing fighters with moderately high subsonic performance and a mixed armament of cannon and rockets.

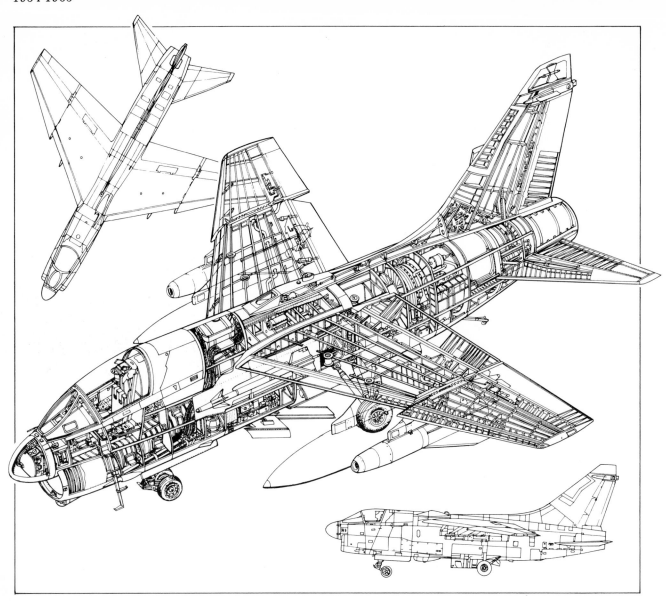

The Vought A-7 multi-role aircraft was modelled on the aerodynamics of the F-8 Crusader fighter, with greater strength and load-carrying capability matched to a turbofan power plant. The wheel is turning full circle with the evolution of a supersonic A-7.

F9F-6 Cougar. More important was the development of the U.S.A.'s first transonic fighter, the North American F-86 Sabre with 35° swept wings. This was designed under the leadership of the two men primarily responsible for the Mustang, and was originally schemed as similar to the straight-winged FJ-1 Fury carrierborne fighter produced to meet a 1944 U.S. Navy requirement. When the results of German research were made available to designers, the new fighter was recast with swept wings, and first flew in October 1947 on the power of an Allison J35 turbojet. The initial production model was the F-86A with a 5,200-lb (2,359-kg) thrust General Electric J47 axial-flow turbojet and an armament of six 0.5-in machine-guns grouped three on each side of the circular nose inlet, which was surmounted by a blister for the ranging radar. The F-86A attained 675 mph (1,086 km/h) at 2,500 ft (760 m), equivalent to Mach 0.89, possessed an initial climb rate of 7,630 ft (2,326 m) per minute and could climb to a service ceiling of 48,300 ft (14,720 m). In December 1950 the F-86A was supplanted on the production line by

the F-86E with an all-flying and power-boosted tailplane and an artificial 'feel' system.

It was these two fighters which fought out the world's first large-scale 'jet-versus-jet' fighter conflict above the Korean War. In general the Soviet fighter was superior at heights above 35,000 ft (10,670 m), but suffered directional stability problems and a tendency to flick into a spin: but the combination of better gunnery aids and the American pilots' superior training provided an almost unbelievable kill ratio superiority of 10.63:1 for the Sabres over the Chinese- and Soviet-flown MiGs. The first encounter between MiGs and Sabres occurred on 17 December 1950, when the F-86As of the 4th Fighter Interceptor Wing destroyed four MiGs for no loss to themselves. Manoeuvring parity with the MiG was achieved by the

Above: The TF-102A was the two-seat conversion and combat proficiency trainer variant of the Convair F-102A interceptor.

Below: The Gloster Javelin FAW.Mk 9 was the ultimate variant of this powerful all-weather fighter.

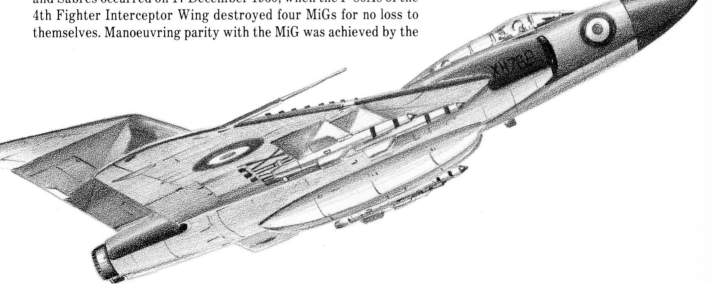

adoption of the extended-chord '6-3' wing on the upengined F-86F that entered service in the spring of 1952. Further development continued, and the Sabre was produced in many variants over the next few years, including the radar-equipped F-86D all-weather interceptor, the F-86F day fighter and the F-86H fighter-bomber.

The Soviets appreciated that the MiG-15's aerodynamic design left much to be desired, and pushed ahead with the MiG-17 (NATO reporting name 'Fresco') which can thus be regarded as the 'definitive MiG-15'. The MiG-17 bore strong similarities to the MiG-15, but possessed finer lines, wings swept at 45° inboard and 42° outboard, and several other aerodynamic improvements. The type was powered by the VK-1 turbojet: the standard engine as used in the MiG-15bis for the initial variants, and the VK-1F rated at 7,451-lb (3,380-kg) afterburning thrust in later models.

The Americans did not parallel this development, but moved straight to a supersonic fighter, the North American F-100 Super

Above: Heavy and comparatively underpowered, the Republic F-84 series always required a long runway and the pilot's prayers that there was no engine failure on take-off.

Left: Great things were expected of the Convair F-102A Delta Dagger, but the type was only modestly supersonic despite the fact that the type was redesigned to incorporate an area-ruled fuselage for reduced drag.

Above: The Lockheed F-94C Starfire was a radar-equipped all-weather interceptor derived from the T-33 two-seat trainer version of the F-80 Shooting Star single-seat fighter.

Below: The U.K.'s finest transonic fighter of the 1950s was the beautiful Hawker Hunter.

Sabre. This was originally planned as a radical development of the Sabre (with the name Sabre 45 to indicate the use of a 45° swept wing) but emerged as a wholly new aeroplane possessing extremely clean overall lines, fitted with an all-flying tailplane, and powered by a Pratt & Whitney J57 turbojet rated at 9,700-lb (4,400-kg) afterburning thrust. The type flew on its maiden flight in May 1953, and began to enter service as the F-100A interceptor with an armament of four 20-mm cannon, the U.S. Air Force having come to the conclusion that the short duration of jet-versus-jet fighter combat offered such fleeting gunfire opportunities that the greater weight and destructive power of cannon shells was superior to the sheer volume of the previous massed batteries of 0.5-in machine-guns. The Super Sabre was genuinely supersonic in level flight, and went on in later marks to become a powerful ground-attack aeroplane.

The Soviet counter to the Super Sabre was the MiG-19, allocated the reporting name 'Farmer' by NATO. There exists uncertainty as to the date of the MiG-19's first flight, so the type may well have been the first supersonic fighter to fly. By any criteria the MiG-19 was a superb achievement in aerodynamic and structural terms. The wings were swept at 55°, and while the problem of wing twist had persuaded the designers of the Super Sabre to adopt inboard ailerons, the Soviet designers produced a remarkably thin wing of such rigidity that outboard ailerons could be used, with all their advantages for higher rates of roll. The first prototype flew, probably in October 1952, with a single Lyulka AL-5 turbojet rated at up to 11,023-lb (5,000-kg) afterburning thrust, but the arrangement accepted for production aircraft was a pair of Tumansky-designed Mikulin AM-5 afterburning turbojets rated at 7,165-lb (3,040-kg) afterburning thrust and exhausting through pen-

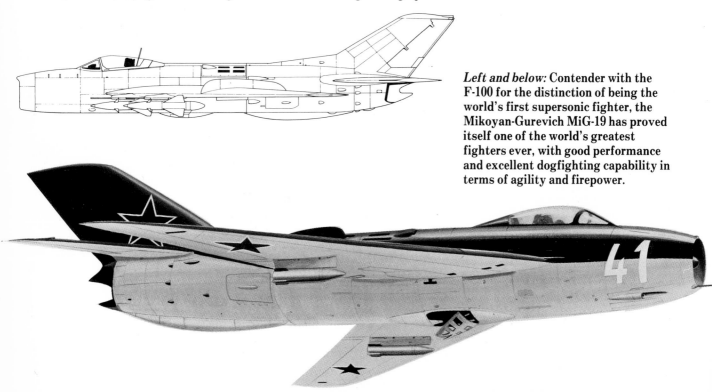

Left and below: Contender with the F-100 for the distinction of being the world's first supersonic fighter, the Mikoyan-Gurevich MiG-19 has proved itself one of the world's greatest fighters ever, with good performance and excellent dogfighting capability in terms of agility and firepower.

Above and right: **In the Douglas F4D Skyray the U.S. Navy had a potent interceptor with supersonic speed and phenomenal rate of climb matched to capable cannon armament.**

nib exhausts in the tail: later marks of the MiG-19 used the Tumansky RD-9 in rating up to the 7,277-lb (3,300-kg) afterburning thrust of the RD-9BF. Armament remained the standard one 37-mm and two 23-mm cannon (later changed to three 30-mm weapons), though the MiG-19PM featured the same primitive installation of four AA-1 'Alkali' beam-riding air-to-air missiles as the MiG-17PFU. The definitive MiG-19S with all-flying tailplane began to enter service in 1954, and the 'Farmer' has remained in widespread service since that time. Western estimates originally rated the type highly, but by the 1960s the MiG-19 was deemed obsolescent in the face of Western fighters with Mach 2 performance and superior air-to-air missile armament. Adherents of this belief were sadly disabused in the Vietnam War, however, when the MiG-19 proved itself able to best these 'advanced' fighters through its powerful cannon armament, excellent agility, and rapid rates of climb and acceleration. The Chinese have continued to produce the type in improved versions for their own use and export, this Shenyang J-6

still being a formidable adversary for all but the latest Western fighters.

While the two major world powers were pushing forward with the development and widespread introduction of these first supersonic fighters, and already preparing their plans for Mach 2 fighters in response to the apparent lessons of the air campaign within the Korean War, other countries were making slower progress. An early contender was Sweden, which in 1951 introduced the Saab J 29 fighter, an extremely tubby pod-and-boom type built round the 5,000-lb (2,272-kg) thrust Svenska Flygmotor RM2, a licence-built version of the de Havilland Ghost 50 centrifugal-flow turbojet. The Swedish fighter's performance was well up to the standards of the day (though firmly subsonic) and was armed with four 20-mm cannon. France also introduced its first jet fighters in this period, the earliest type to reach operational service being the Ouragan designed by Dassault, as Bloch had been renamed after the

Above: The North American F-100 Super Sabre was a great technical achievement and a useful fighter, but ultimately proved to have less going for it than its exact contemporary, the MiG-19. However, the type did prove useful in the Vietnam War as a ground-attack aircraft of great resistance to battle damage.

war in celebration of the name adopted by Marcel Bloch to hide his Jewish origins in that war. The Ouragan was used successfully as a fighter-bomber (most notably by India and Israel), but replaced in French service by the Dassault Mystère IIC, which was a reworking of the Ouragan with swept wings. The Mystère IIC was then replaced by the definitive Mystère IVA with the 7,716-lb (3,500-kg) thrust Hispano-Suiza Verdon 350, a licence-built version of the Rolls-Royce Tay centrifugal-flow turbojet.

The Vampire's British replacement appeared in 1952 as the de Havilland Venom, retaining the same basic configuration as the Vampire in refined form, powered by a 4,850-lb (220-kg) thrust Ghost turbojet and armed with four 20-mm cannon. The Venom was

Below: The McDonnell F-101 Voodoo was schemed as an escort fighter, but proved better in the missile-carrying air-defence role, and then in the operational reconnaissance task.

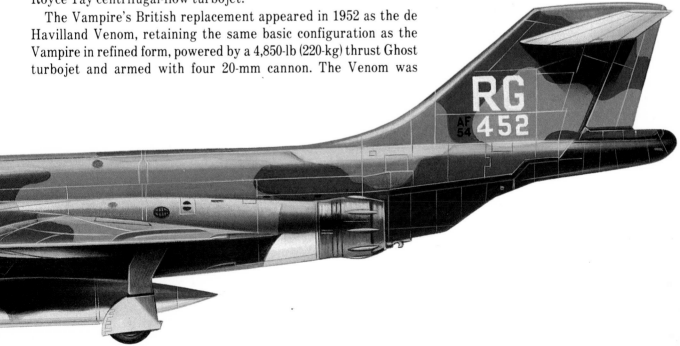

Left: With two Rolls-Royce Avon turbojets and transonic performance, the Supermarine Scimitar F.Mk 1 was a naval aeroplane equally at home in the interceptor and attack roles.

Left: The Dassault Etendard IV-M can be considered the French counterpart to the Scimitar, though powered by only a single engine and thus carrying smaller loads over shorter ranges.

obsolescent as a single-seat fighter when it was introduced, however, and was more usefully employed as a fighter-bomber with 2,000 lb (907 kg) of bombs or rockets. The type was also developed with greater power as a night-fighter and as a naval all-weather fighter. A contemporary single-seat naval fighter was the Hawker Sea Hawk with the 5,100-lb (2,313-kg) thrust Rolls-Royce Nene turbojet in the centre fuselage, drawing in air through lateral inlets and exhausting through bifurcated pipes in the trailing edge of each wing root.

These British fighters were useful in a limited fashion, but their greatest significance lies in the breathing space and experience they gave to industry for the development of the Hawker Hunter, which began to enter service in the second half of 1954. Earlier British jet fighters had been fitted with unswept wings and large-diameter centrifugal-flow engines, but Camm and his design team introduced

Right: The A 32A was the attack aeroplane from which the two-seat Saab J 32 two-seat all-weather/night fighter was developed.

Above: **The Dassault-Breguet Mirage F1 is still an effective multi-role fighter, the type having proved a commercial success in French and overseas service as a result of the manufacturer's willingness to develop specific models suited to different purses and different requirements.**

in the Hunter a fully-fledged transonic fighter with wings swept at 40°, an axial-flow turbojet and a troublesome installation of four 30-mm cannon with a breech/magazine section that winched down for rapid reloading. There was indecision in high places about which of the two available engines, both of them highly promising, was to be used, and the Hunter was initially brought into service in two main forms, the Hunter F.Mk 1 with the Rolls-Royce Avon and the Hunter F.Mk 2 with the Armstrong Siddeley Sapphire. Eventually the Avon-powered version was standardised, and evolved via the Hunter F.Mk 4 with additional internal fuel (always too limited in British fighters) and underwing provision for disposable weapons or more fuel. The Hunter reached its apogee as a fighter in its F.Mk 6 form with the 'full-bore' Avon 200 series engine and extended-chord outer wing panels for improved manoeuvrability at high speed. The Hunter has proved itself a well-loved and versatile machine, and

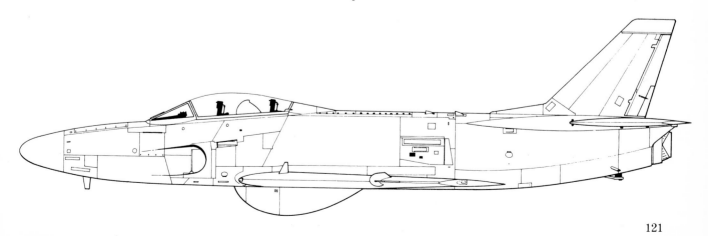

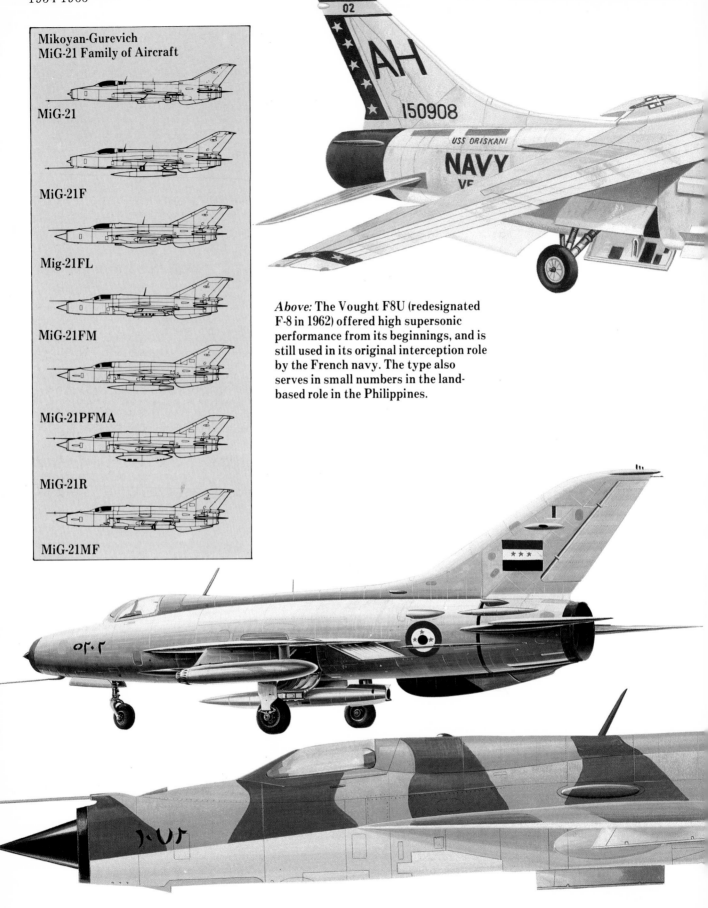

Mikoyan-Gurevich MiG-21 Family of Aircraft

MiG-21

MiG-21F

Mig-21FL

MiG-21FM

MiG-21PFMA

MiG-21R

MiG-21MF

Above: The Vought F8U (redesignated F-8 in 1962) offered high supersonic performance from its beginnings, and is still used in its original interception role by the French navy. The type also serves in small numbers in the land-based role in the Philippines.

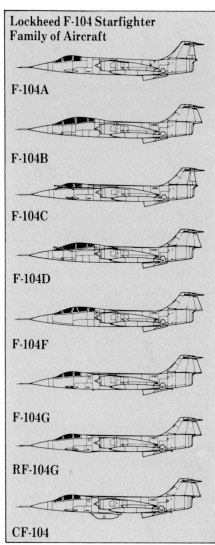

Lockheed F-104 Starfighter Family of Aircraft

F-104A

F-104B

F-104C

F-104D

F-104F

F-104G

RF-104G

CF-104

survives in some numbers to the present day. When the type's age began to catch up with it in the pure fighter role, the Hunter was further developed as an exceptional fighter-bomber and reconnaissance aircraft, culminating in the classic Hunter FGA.Mk 9 variant. The Hunter's main rival in the early stages of its life was the Supermarine Swift, but this enjoyed only a short service life because of intractable aerodynamic problems.

The early 1950s was a period in which the bomber armed with free-fall nuclear weapons was the primary strategic threat, and the air forces of the world's major powers placed great emphasis on the development of all-weather fighters, capable of day and night operations, able to tackle such threats either independently or using

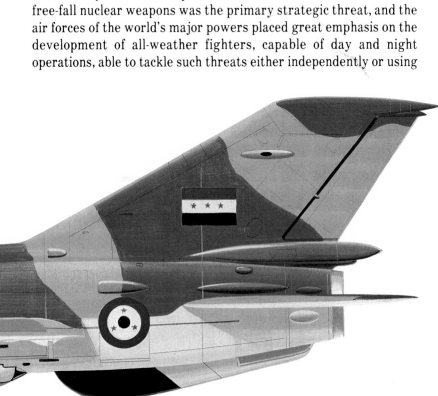

Left: The Mikoyan-Gurevich MiG-21 has been built in larger numbers than any other warplane since World War II, and though at first very limited in capability (MiG-21F, far left) has been extensively developed in powerplant, radar and weapons to make it an effective dual-role fighter and ground-attack type.

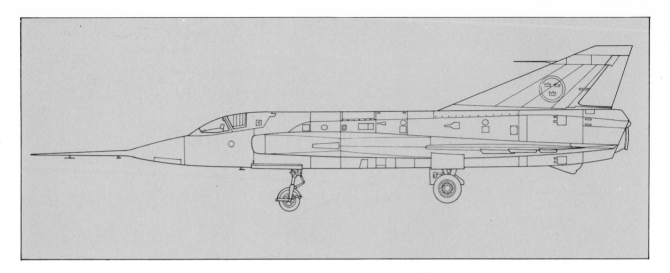

Above: A contemporary of the English Electric Lightning, the fascinating Saab J 35 Draken used only one Rolls-Royce Avon afterburning turbojet to the Lightning's two, yet secured much the same performance except in climb, and carried a heavier armament.

ground-controlled interception techniques. The demands of this role were great, including a two-man crew, radar, comprehensive flight and navigation equipment and heavy weapons, and this generally dictated a large airframe and two engines. The way forward had been indicated by the F-94 Starfire, but the next step was the extraordinary Northrop F-89 Scorpion, which appeared in 1951 as a a virtual pod-and-boom type with two Allison J35 axial-flow turbojets in a semi-podded installation in the sides of the lower fuselage, nose radar and an armament of six 20-mm cannon. Later models epitomise the growth in capability for this role in the next few years: the F-89C added provision for 16 5-in (127-mm) unguided rockets under the wings, the F-89C became the major model with the cannon deleted and pods for 104 2.75-in (70-mm) unguided rockets (fired automatically by the Hughes fire-control system) added at the wingtips, the F-89H featured an armament of six Hughes Falcon air-to-air missiles, and the F-89J added the Hughes M12 autotracking system and provision for two examples of the Douglas Genie unguided rocket, whose nuclear warhead was detonated by the fire-control system when the target was inside the lethal radius.

Slightly farther to the north, the Canadians were also concerned with the possibility of Soviet intrusion over the Arctic, and

Above left and above: The mighty F-105 Thunderchief was the last combat aircraft developed by Republic, and was a typically massive strike fighter with high supersonic performance and great warload. The type's nickname of 'Thud' aptly summed up this monster.

developed their own all-weather interceptor as the Avro Canada CF-100 Canuck. This appeared in 1953 with 6,500-lb (2,948 kg) thrust Orenda turbojets and enormous fuel capacity for greater range. The main armament was a total of 104 2.75-in unguided rockets fired by the Canuck's onboard radar fire-control system. The U.K. was also concerned with the threat of the strategic bomber, and produced the Gloster Javelin which appeared in 1956. The British aerodynamic solution was different to those of the Americans and Canadians, being a massive delta-winged aircraft with a delta horizontal tail carried on top of the vertical tail. Power was provided by two 8,000-lb (3,629-kg) Sapphire turbojets, and the main armament was four 30-mm Aden cannon in the wings, later revised to a pair of such cannon and four de Havilland Firestreak air-to-air missiles.

The Soviet counter to these types was the Yakovlev Yak-25, which was allocated the NATO reporting name 'Flashlight'. This appeared in 1955, and featured highly-swept flying surfaces, two 5,732-lb (2,600-kg) thrust Tumansky RD-9 turbojets, a massive radar system, and an armament of two powerful 37-mm cannon. The French Sud-Ouest Vautour bore many similarities to the Yak-25 in overall configuration and, like the Soviet fighter, was carried on a bicycle landing gear arrangement (retracting into the fuselage) with stabilising outriggers.

As these single- and two-seat fighters were being developed, the major powers were digesting the implications of the Korean War and laying plans for their future fighters. In the U.S.A. the lessons of Korea seemed to confirm the need for three basic types: a single-seat interceptor possessing phenomenal rate of climb and speed at the expense of agility, a single-seat all-weather air-defence fighter with Mach 2 performance and a high-quality missile armament optimised for use with a ground controller and/or onboard fire-control system, and a two-seat escort and penetration fighter with good flight performance (though not as high as that of the single-seaters) coupled with long range and substantial armament.

The interceptor requirement resulted in the Lockheed F-104 Starfighter, often dubbed the 'manned missile' as in layout it is a massive fuselage (accommodating the pilot, electronics, powerplant and fuel system, and landing gear) combined with very small but almost straight wings and a substantial T-tail. The powerplant is the now-legendary General Electric J79 turbojet with full afterburning for a thrust of 14,800 lb (6,713 kg), and after a trouble-prone development period the F-104A began to enter service in 1958 with an armament of one multi-barrel 20-mm cannon in the fuselage and two Sidewinder air-to-air missiles at the wingtips. However, the type's operational career with the U.S.A.F. was short, for it was soon appreciated that the basic concept was flawed and that the Starfighter was thus too limited in capability. The type was developed further as the F-104C fighter-bomber, but the Starfighter's career would have ended there but for the adoption of the type by a consortium of other N.A.T.O. nations as their standard tactical aircraft. This resulted in the multi-national F-104G variant

Below: Developed from the P.1 research aircraft, the English Electric Lightning featured the unusual arrangement of twin engines arranged vertically within the deep fuselage and fed via a large circular nose inlet.

Below: The ultimate fighter development of the original McDonnell Phantom II series is the F-4E with an inbuilt cannon, greater power, upgraded electronics and a number of aerodynamic improvements.

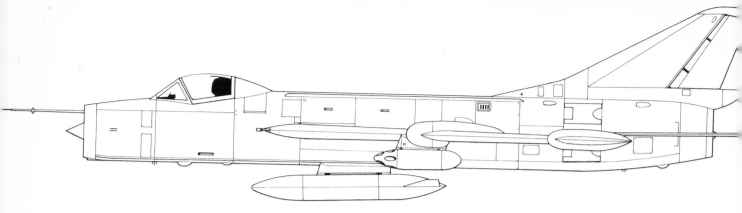

with a stiffened fuselage, manoeuvring flaps, a comprehensive suite of advanced electronics, and provision for a modest but highly varied offensive warload. The ultimate development of this concept is the Italian Aeritalia F-104S with provision for medium-range semi-active radar homing missiles.

The naval counterparts to the Starfighter (but by no means its equivalent) were the Douglas F4D Skyray and Vought F8U Crusader. The Skyray was introduced in 1956 as a lightweight interceptor with the capability to go just supersonic in level flight, but truly prodigious climb performance including a time of 1 minute 51 seconds to 39,370 ft (12,000 m). Unlike the earlier but similar Vought F7U Cutlass, which had been a flying wing with twin vertical tail surfaces on very short booms aft of the wings, the Skyray was a delta with a single vertical tail surface. Power was provided by a 14,500-lb (6,577-kg) afterburning thrust Pratt & Whitney J57 turbojet, and the armament comprised four 20-mm cannon and/or missiles. The Crusader was a heavier aeroplane of conventional layout though featuring an unusual variable-incidence wing so that the aeroplane could approach the carrier with its fuselage in the level rather than nose-tip attitude. Armed with four 20-mm cannon plus two or four Sidewinder missiles, the Crusader was powered by a 16,200-lb (7,348-kg) afterburning thrust J57 and could reach very nearly Mach 2 in level flight.

The air-defence concept produced two important types in the forms of the McDonnell F3H Demon for the U.S. Navy and the Convair F-102 Delta Dagger for the U.S.A.F., both types being introduced in 1956. Each was modestly supersonic and armed with

Above: Designed as the Soviet counter to the American F-100 and F-101 heavy fighters, the Sukhoi Su-7 was developed most effectively as a ground-attack type with enormous ability to withstand battle damage and deliver its weapons accurately.

Below: France's primary fighter of the 1960s was the Dassault Mirage III, which has genuine Mach 2 performance. The type was designed for a mixed powerplant of one afterburning turbojet and one SEPR 841 liquid-propellant rocket to increase ceiling to about 100,000 ft (30,480 m). The rocket has seldom been used, its volume being more usefully employed for additional jet fuel.

Dassault Mirage III Family of Aircraft

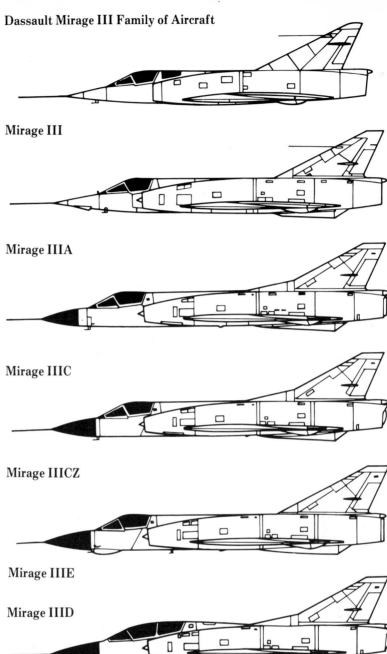

Mirage III

Mirage IIIA

Mirage IIIC

Mirage IIICZ

Mirage IIIE

Mirage IIID

Right: **In common with other modern fighters, the Mirage III has been produced in several forms with revised features for differing capabilities.**

air-to-air missiles (four infra-red homing Sidewinders or semi-active radar homing Sparrows on the F3H, and six infra-red/semi-active radar homing Falcons on the F-102), and the F-102 had a capable fire-control system. However, both types proved disappointing in service, and were supplanted by more capable designs, the F3H by the superlative McDonnell Douglas F4H Phantom II and the F-102 by the Convair F-106 Delta Dart.

The long-range fighter concept produced two U.S.A.F. types, the McDonnell F-101 Voodoo introduced in 1957 and the Republic F-105 Thunderchief introduced in 1959. The Voodoo was schemed as an escort fighter with very long range, but was accepted for service as a long-range air-defence weapon with two 18,000-lb (8,165-kg)

Above and right: The Northrop F-5 series of lightweight fighters was produced to meet the needs of those American allies which could not afford or did not need the highly supersonic fighters used by the U.S. forces. The result was an extremely cost-effective design that needed little maintenance or support from a high-technology base, yet offered modestly supersonic performance with useful weapon capability.

afterburning thrust J57s, Mach 1.85 performance and an armament of four 20-mm cannon and three Falcon air-to-air missiles. The type served also (and more successfully) in the reconnaissance role. The Thunderchief was an altogether more potent aeroplane schemed as replacement for the F-100 in the nuclear strike role. As such it was powered by the 26,500-lb (12,020-kg) afterburning thrust Pratt & Whitney J75 turbojet, and was capable of Mach 2 +. However, despite its fighter designation the type was really an attack/strike aircraft.

It was these American fighters that set the technological standard against which other fighters must inevitably be judged. And in the U.S.S.R. and Europe there had been much development in the second half of the 1950s. The British effort resulted in the introduction of the Supermarine Scimitar in 1958, the de Havilland Sea Vixen in 1959 and the English Electric Lightning in 1960. The first pair were carrierborne aircraft, the former a Mach 0.95 multi-role fighter with two 11,250-lb (5,103-kg) thrust Avon 200 turbojets and an armament of four 30-mm cannon plus Sidewinder missiles or 8,000 lb of disposable stores, while the latter was a transonic all-weather interceptor of the proven de Havilland design configuration and powered by two Avon 200s to carry an armament of four Firestreak missiles plus 28 2-in (51-mm) rockets in a retractable belly pack. Such an armament was widely used by the fighters of this period, the idea being that the target area could be blanketed by a mass of powerful weapons in a single cost-effective salvo. The Lightning was an altogether more capable fighter, a Mach 2 land-based machine designed to use two vertically-disposed Avon 200s, each rated at 14,430-lb (6,545-kg) afterburning thrust, for exceptional rate of climb and ceiling with two 30-mm cannon plus two Firestreak missiles or 48 2-in unguided rockets. The Lightning has undergone considerable development, and is being phased out of service only in the late 1980s. It is interesting to note, though, that this first (and only) supersonic fighter of purely British design displayed the two failings that have beset British fighters since the 1930s, namely short range and light armament.

The French effort produced the Dassault Super Mystère B2 in 1957. This was essentially the Mystère IVA revised with cleaner lines and a 9,700-lb (4,400-kg) thrust SNECMA Atar 101G turbojet for marginally supersonic performance with an armament of two 30-mm cannon and a retractable pack of 35 unguided rockets. From this the French moved to the delta-winged Dassault Mirage III with Mach 2 performance provided by the 14,076-lb (6,385-kg) afterburning thrust Atar 9B turbojet, and an armament of two 30-mm cannon and an increasingly heavy and diverse assortment of disposable stores as the type was developed into a true multi-role fighter. The Mirage III was widely exported, and is still in world-wide service. The type has also undergone development as the Mirage 5 clear-weather and Mirage 50 multi-role fighters, and local modification to improve its overall capabilities have resulted in the totally revised Israel Aircraft Industries Kfir (lion cub) with the American J79 engine, wholly modern electronics and canard foreplanes to improve agility, and in the upgraded Atlas Cheetah from South Africa, which resembles the Kfir but has the original Atar turbojet. The naval contemporary of the Mirage III was the swept-wing Dassault Etendard IV-M with the 9,700-lb thrust Atar 8 and an armament of the two 30-mm cannon and an assortment of disposable loads. In 1976 the upgraded Super Etendard (super standard) appeared with important electronic improvements and the 11,023-lb (5,000-kg) thrust Atar 8K-50 turbojet.

France's next step was the Dassault Mirage F1, which appeared in 1966 with the 15,873-lb (7,200-kg) afterburning thrust Atar 9K-50 and a high-set swept wing for considerably greater sustained agility than the Mirage III without any loss of overall performance. The Mirage F1 sports the standard pair of 30-mm cannon plus a maximum disposable load of 8,818 lb (4,000 kg) including a maximum of five air-to-air missiles. Like the preceding Mirage III/5 series, the Mirage F1 has been developed in alternative forms optimised for all-weather or clear-weather interception and attack, and this

Below: The Sukhoi Su-21 'Flagon' is a dedicated high-level interceptor intended for use within the Soviet concept of an air-defence network using ground-controlled interception techniques.

availability of variously priced alternatives has promoted the type's success as an export weapon.

Sweden was also producing fighters matched to its own particular requirements: the Saab Lansen (lance) appeared in 1958, and though primarily developed as the A 32 attack aeroplane, was also produced as the J 32B with the 15,212-lb (6,900-kg) afterburning thrust RM6B (the Swedish version of the Avon 200) in the role of all-weather fighter with four 30-mm cannon and Sidewinder missiles. The Saab Draken (dragon) appeared in 1959, and was also produced in multiple variants. The fighter was the J 35, and this too was powered by the RM6. The result of this afterburning powerplant combined with an exceptional airframe with double-delta wings was western Europe's first genuinely supersonic fighter, which has been extensively developed for service into the 1980s with an armament of one or two 30-mm cannon plus four missiles (Sidewinders and/or Falcons).

Two trim but little recognised lightweight fighters were also developed as the Fiat G.91 of 1959 and the Folland Gnat of 1960. Each was powered by a single Bristol Orpheus turbojet in the 5,000-lb thrust class and, while the Italian machine was developed as a fighter-bomber, the British fighter was used mainly as an advanced trainer. The Gnat did serve as a fighter with Finland and

Below: The Fiat G.91 resulted from a NATO requirement for a lightweight attack fighter, but in the event was bought only by Italy and West Germany, though the type is now operated by Portugal.

India, the latter producing a developed variant as the HAL Ajeet.

The Soviet assessment of the Korean War resulted in a series of conclusions somewhat different from those found by the Americans. The Soviets stressed agility in their short-range interceptor, and this produced the very widely used Mikoyan-Gurevich MiG-21, dubbed 'Fishbed' by N.A.T.O. and using a series of Tumansky afterburning turbojets in successive variants. The MiG-21 is a tailed delta and first flew in 1955. The early models were severely limited in armament and performance (in most respects other than speed, which was Mach 2), but development has turned the MiG-21 into a useful and highly affordable supersonic fighter with a two-barrel 23-mm cannon and four air-to-air missiles. The MiG-21 has also been produced in China as the Xian J-7, with further development resulting in the much-improved F-7M Airguard with Western electronics, and the considerably revised Shenyang J-8 with twin-engined powerplant.

The nearest Western equivalents to the MiG-21 are the two basic variants of the Northrop F-5 series, powered by two General Electric J85 afterburning turbojets. The F-5A Freedom Fighter first flew in 1959 as a moderate-performance fighter suitable for export to those American allies requiring a Mach 2 fighter, and has Mach 1.4 performance with an armament of two 20-mm cannon and some 5,000 lb of disposable stores. The upengined F-5E Tiger II flew in 1972, and offers Mach 1.6 performance with the same fixed armament plus 7,000 lb (3,175 kg) of disposable stores.

For air-defence the Soviets introduced the medium-weight Sukhoi Su-9 and Su-11 'Fishpot' from 1956, succeeded in the later 1960s by the Su-15 and Su-21 'Flagon' series with speed increased from Mach

Above: **The variable-geometry Grumman F-14A Tomcat is a large fighter in every respect, and offers unrivalled interception capability at very long ranges thanks to its combination of high-power electronics and Phoenix air-to-air missiles.**

1.8 to Mach 2.3. And for all-weather interception the Soviets in 1951 introduced the massive Tupolev Tu-28 'Fiddler' with two 27,006-lb (12,250-kg) afterburning thrust turbojets for Mach 1.75 performance and carrying four giant air-to-air missiles.

The Americans were still forging ahead, and at this time decided that while there remained no basic fault in the overall parameters of the programme they had been pursuing since the end of the Korean War, the time was now ripe for further development of the fighter as a long-range weapon system carrying a powerful radar and fire-control system matched to an increased battery of missiles. The updated concept thus emphasised improved electronic and flight performance, but the abandonment of the gun, now seen as an irrelevance when the decisive weapon was the missile. The first results of this concept were the F-106 Delta Dart for the U.S.A.F. and the F4H Phantom for the U.S. Navy, together with the incredible Grumman F-14 Tomcat, also for the U.S. Navy. The era of the fighter as missile-carrier was about to dawn.

It might be more accurate, perhaps, to say that the missile-carrier's era was apparently about to dawn, for the Americans had oversimplified their thinking as a result of too great a belief in the capabilities of technology pure and simple. In theory, therefore, the Americans were right: but what they had failed to appreciate were agility combined with cannon power (a factor never lost on the Soviets) and the inevitable failure of sophisticated systems to work as advertised. This meant that the new American fighters were excellent on paper (and sometimes approached this promise when operating for short times under ideal conditions) but in practice severely limited in a number of vital tactical features.

1966-1990
The Modern Fighter

By the mid-1950s it was apparent that advances in electronic technology and miniaturisation were approaching the point at which it might be possible to regard the fighter as a missile platform rather than a fighting aircraft in its own right. This hypothesis seemed to offer the possibility of producing highly capable machines of comparatively limited agility but great speed, rate of climb and endurance for the express purpose of carrying a powerful combination of radar and its associated fire-control system to a position where long-range missiles could be launched against a target detected by the fighter's own radar. This attractive hypothesis apparently provided the chance for already expensive fighters to be fitted with just as expensive electronic systems in a manner made cost-effective by their reduced chances of being downed: they would be able to detect and destroy attackers at long range, and would in any event have a self-defence capability in the form of short-range infra-red homing missiles to complement the main battery of semi-active or even active radar homing offensive missiles.

It was in this type of situation that the great McDonnell F4H (later McDonnell Douglas F-4) Phantom II appeared in 1960. The basic airframe was already under development as the AH-1 carrierborne strike and attack aircraft when the decision was made to create a new all-weather fighter optimised for the fleet defence role with complete autonomy of operation from its parent carrier. This was the first time that such a capability had been envisaged.

The aircraft that emerged from this programme has become a classic: a large fuselage with radar in the nose, the crew of two seated in tandem, the two engines located side-by-side in the centre fuselage, and an empennage set comparatively high (in typical McDonnell fashion) to keep it clear of the jet exhausts. The large wing is of almost delta shape, with sharply upswept outer panels, and the two halves of the slab tailplane are angled sharply down. Performance was fixed at more than Mach 2, and to provide the required power the F4H was designed round two 16,150-lb (7,326-kg) afterburning thrust General Electric J79 turbojets supplied with air through lateral trunks with inlets that are automatically controlled for optimum airflow at all altitudes and all speeds. Yet the fighter was intended for carrier operation, and thus needed low take-off and landing speed, which was provided by blown leading- and trailing-edge flaps combined with powerful conventional controls and spoilers. The armament was fixed at four long-range Sparrow air-to-

air missiles, carried in a low-drag installation semi-recessed in the belly of the area-ruled fuselage, and four short-range Sidewinders: this makes a striking contrast with the armament of contemporaries such as the English Electric Lightning, which sported just two air-to-air missiles in addition to its cannon armament. The F4H had no gun armament.

From the beginning of the flight test programme the F4H proved its exceptional performance at all altitudes, setting world records for high- and low-level speed, climb and ceiling. In service the type was also impressive, and an unusual accolade was a steadily increasing U.S. Air Force demand for the Phantom, one of the very few occasions on which a navel combat aeroplane has been adopted by the air force. Few modifications were demanded in the initial air force model, which was required to fill a severe tactical gap in the U.S.A.F.'s front-line inventory, but since that time the Phantom II has been produced in many forms to meet differing requirements in the air-to-air and air-to-surface roles.

The Phantom was soon blooded in the Vietnam War, and it was here that some of the basic deficiencies in the U.S. fighter concept began to appear when Mach 2 Phantoms were occasionally downed

Above: **The IAI Kfir-C7 is a radical Israeli development of the French Mirage III. Israel started the programme in case France should embargo further weapon deliveries (an event that took place in 1973), first producing a Mirage 'clone' as the Nesher (eagle) which was exported as the Dagger, and then moving onto the Kfir with the American J79 afterburning turbojet and Israeli electronics, before moving onto the Kfir-C2 with canard foreplanes and then the Kfir-C7 with a completely updated electronic suite.**

by MiG-19s of the North Vietnamese air force. It was soon appreciated by the Americans that not all combats would be stand-off engagements dominated by missiles, which in any event proved far less effective than had been anticipated: in short-range combat; the Phantom was at a disadvantage for its lack of manoeuvrability, a fact that was emphasised in dogfights, where the Phantom's lack of a cannon proved itself an enormous tactical disadvantage. And once an engagement had started, the Phantom soon lost its potential edge in speed, while the MiG-19's higher acceleration often proved an advantage. A pod carrying a 20-mm multi-barrel cannon reduced the effect of the Phantom's lack of inbuilt armament, but such an installation was not as effective as an inbuilt weapon and from the U.S.A.F.'s F-4E variant the nose was revised to accommodate a 20-mm Vulcan multi-barrel cannon in a low-drag installation of minimal vibration and thus greater accuracy in comparison with the podded cannon. The lack of close-in manoeuvrability was reduced by the introduction of leading-edge slats on the outer panels of the wings, and slots on the leading edges of the tailplane. Power was also successively improved, and later models featured additional fuel and improved electronics of various kinds. British Phantoms

Above: The range of weapons available to the modern fighter is well displayed by this layout in front of an IAI Kfir-C2. The assortment includes air-to-air and air-to-surface weapons, the latter of both the 'dumb' unguided and 'smart' guided types.

Above: The Mikoyan-Gurevich MiG-23 'Flogger' is the classic example of Soviet swing-wing design to produce a tactical fighter with high performance but good range and the ability to operate from short runways on semi-prepared forward airfields.

have Rolls-Royce Spey afterburning turbofan engines, and other countries are upgrading their surviving aircraft with more modern electronics to maintain the Phantom II as a viable air-combat type into the next decade.

Whereas the fighters of World War II and the interim period immediately after it had often been used for close support of ground forces, especially when a newer mark of the basic aeroplane had emerged to assume the primary air-combat role, recent fighters have been produced more generally as dual-role fighter and close-support/attack (or fighter-bomber) aircraft. The conversion of fighters to the fighter-bomber role was comparatively simple when all that was required was the installation (sometimes in the field) of the necessary racks and release system for free-fall weapons or unguided rockets, and this basic concept was retained (often through the installation of the necessary wiring during initial manufacture) into the 1950s. Thereafter the increasing sophistication and growing number of possible ground-attack weapon types (especially after the advent of guided weapons) has dictated that the fighter be designed from the outset with the appropriate systems, turning the fighter into a dual-capability or even multi-role type according to the weapons and sensors carried. Naturally enough, such a practice also increases the cost-effectiveness of individual aircraft types by reducing the number of different combat types that need be kept in the inventory. On the other side of the coin, however, the designer and operator service must ensure that this concept does not produce a front-line aeroplane that is 'jack of all trades but master of none': air combat is at the cutting edge of military aircraft technology, and sacrifices to dual capability can be purchased only at the considerable expense of pure 'fightability', which in turn increases losses.

The problem did not arise with the Convair F-106 Delta Dart, which was schemed as the definitive version of the F-102 Delta Dagger as the genuinely Mach 2 air-defence fighter that had been desired all along. The F-106 first flew in 1956 and began to enter service in 1959, and was dedicated to its single role within the overall context of a ground-controlled air-defence network for the North American continent, using large numbers of radars and computerised control centres to generate an all-embracing capability against individual or mass intruders. The primary fighters employed in this system were the McDonnell F-101 Voodoo, which was phased out of the role comparatively early in its career, and the F-106. This served as North American Air Defense

Below: The SEPECAT Jaguar is a fascinating Anglo-French strike and reconnaissance fighter with modest performance but excellent weapon-carriage and weapon-delivery capablities.

Command's main fighter for some 20 years, only latterly being supplemented by the Phantom II and later aircraft such as the F-15 and F-16. The Delta Dart was not intended for dogfighting, so the choice of a large delta wing and area-ruled fuselage provided the right blend of performance (including a maximum speed of Mach 2.3 and long range) and weapon carriage capability. The type was planned as a missile carrier, with a load of two Genie nuclear-tipped rockets or four Falcon conventionally-armed missiles carried in a lower-fuselage weapon bay for minimum drag, but the lessons of the Vietnam War urged a revision and in-service Delta Darts were retrofitted with the standard internal 20-mm multi-barrel cannon.

The Phantom dominated its field for about 10 years, and it was only from the late 1960s that the U.S. forces began in earnest to search for a replacement. The U.S. Navy was at first constrained by political pressures into accepting the development of a naval version of the General Dynamics F-111 strike aircraft, a large and highly advanced variable-geometry aeroplane under development for the U.S.A.F., but when the F-111B emerged in prototype form it was clearly far too heavy a machine and was thankfully cancelled by the navy. Grumman had been the subcontractor mainly responsible for the F-111B, and used its experience with the variable-geometry layout to offer in replacement the mighty Grumman Tomcat, accepted as the F-14 with the radar fire-control and armament systems (the Hughes AWG-9 and Hughes AIM-54 Phoenix respectively) developed for the F-111B. This weapons system picked up where that of the Phantom II left off, giving yet longer-reached defensive air capability for U.S. Navy battle groups. The radar can detect targets at a range of more than 125 miles (200 km), track several of these simultaneously and engage six of them with its complement of six long-range air-to-air missiles, which use a combination of inertial and semi-active radar homing for the mid-course phase of their flights before switching on their small but powerful active radars for the terminal phase of the attack. The Phoenix provides the Tomcat with its long-range punch, but this highly versatile machine can also carry the Sparrow medium-range and Sidewinder short-range missiles, and is also fitted with a 20-mm multi-barrel cannon. The Tomcat is not designed for such situations, but can give a very good account of itself despite its size.

It is worth noting, moreover, that another feature of the Vietnam War was the political as well as purely military need to secure positive visual identification of a potential target as definitely hostile before a missile was launched against it: the combination of long-range radar and short-range radar was thus of little use in that conflict, to the severe tactical disadvantage of Sparrow-fitted fighters. Modern American fighters, including the Tomcat, now frequently sport a special TV camera system to allow such positive long-range visual identification of the target: the system can also be used for target detection and tracking, providing a back-up system for the radar.

The Tomcat first flew in 1970, and its weapon system soon proved itself far superior to that of any other fighter in range and

Below: Multiple capabilities are a hallmark of modern aircraft, and the British Aerospace Hawk is a good example of the trend. Though conceived as an advanced trainer, this nimble performer can carry 6,800 lb (3,084 kg) of stores in the ground-attack role, and in the T.Mk 1A variant has a secondary air-defence role with a pair of Sidewinder air-to-air missiles. The basic type is also being developed in two single-seat variants optimised for the attack task.

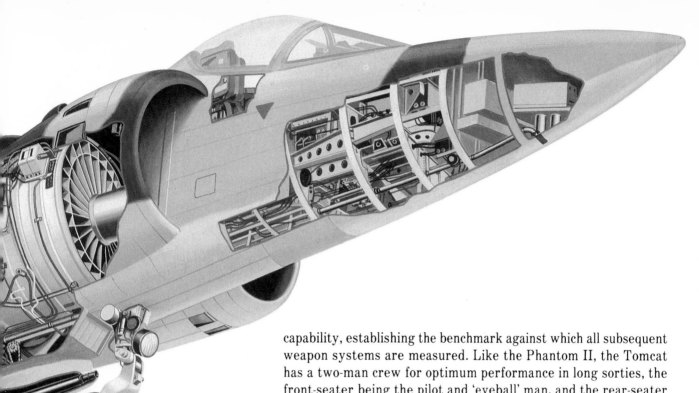

Above: The British Aerospace Harrier was designed for the close-support role. But the Harrier's cannon armament can be supplemented with Sidewinder air-to-air missiles, giving additional air-to-air punch to an aeroplane of almost incredible flight agility when it uses thrust-vectoring to complement the effect of its conventional flight controls.

capability, establishing the benchmark against which all subsequent weapon systems are measured. Like the Phantom II, the Tomcat has a two-man crew for optimum performance in long sorties, the front-seater being the pilot and 'eyeball' man, and the rear-seater the weapon system operator and tactical controller up to the point an engagement begins. The Tomcat's variable-geometry wing provides for excellent performance in all flight regimes: the spread position offers maximum range in the cruising mode (more than 2,000 miles/3,220 km), and low speed for take-off and landing, while the swept position provides maximum performance when required, including a top speed of over Mach 2.34. Current variants of the Tomcat use a powerplant inherited from the F-111, in the form of two 20,900-lb (9,840-kg) afterburning thrust Pratt & Whitney TF30 turbofans. This engine was not designed for fighter use, and in consequence has never been more than adequate in the F-14A first production model. Grumman is now developing an F-14C version with the far more suitable General Electric F110 turbofan, which is rated at 29,000-lb (13,154-kg) afterburning thrust. This will improve performance dramatically, and the opportunity is also being taken to upgrade the fighter's electronics to a fully digital standard for first-rate fighter capability into the next century.

The implications of the Vietnam War were of more direct interest to the U.S.A.F., which also required a replacement for the Phantom II. Given the U.S.A.F.'s roles, a single replacement type was impractical: what emerged, therefore, were the McDonnell Douglas F-15 Eagle air-superiority fighter and the General Dynamics F-16 Fighting Falcon air-combat fighter. In many respects the Eagle can be considered successor to the Phantom II, though advances in electronics have made it possible for the Eagle to do more with a one-man crew than the Phantom II could achieve with two. The Eagle first flew in 1972, and has good manoeuvrability for its size, resulting mainly from the advanced aerodynamics, the large and lightly-loaded wing, and the high thrust-to-weight ratio provided by two 25,000-lb (11,340-kg) afterburning thrust Pratt & Whitney F100 turbofans. This means that the Eagle is perhaps twice as good as the

143

Phantom II in climb rate, acceleration and turn radius, and also offers Mach 2.5+ performance together with great range and ceiling. Matched to the highly capable radar is the standard armament of one 20-mm multi-barrel cannon (the intended 25-mm weapon having failed to materialise) plus four medium-range Sparrow and four short-range Sidewinder missiles, to be replaced eventually by the AIM-120 AMRAAM and AIM-132 ASRAAM respectively. And in its secondary attack role the Eagle can carry up to 16,000 lb (7,257 kg) of disposable stores. The type has been upgraded as the F-15C with enhanced electronics and additional fuel (the latter in strap-on conformal tanks on the side of the two engine trunks) and additional capability is about to be provided to the U.S.A.F. by the development of the F-15E Strike Eagle with yet more electronic improvement and provision for 24,000 lb (10,885 kg) of disposable weapons in this attack-optimised variant. The design is still full of life, and current development is centred on vectoring engine nozzles to reduce take-off and landing run.

The Fighting Falcon first flew in 1974, and is a supremely agile dogfighter optimised for battlefield operations. The lessons of the Vietnam War indicated firmly that such fighters did not need Mach

Below: The Dassault-Breguet Mirage 2000 is France's premier fighter, an extremely impressive type with good performance in all flight regimes thanks to its powerful engine and 'fly-by-wire' computer-run control system, which turns the pilot's control column movement into the most effective possible deflections of the moving control surfaces within the aerodynamic and structural limits of the airframe.

2+ performance and, while no slouch, the Fighting Falcon is designed not so much for outright maximums of performance, but rather for the more important tactical considerations such as climb rate, turn rate and acceleration. The pilot lies under a completely clear canopy in a semi-reclined position that allows him to withstand the high g forces generated by the fighter's superb agility. Control is no longer effected via a central column, but via a right-hand controller working through a computer and 'fly-by-wire' system to wring every last degree of agility out of the elegant airframe, which is powered by a single 25,000-lb afterburning thrust F100 turbofan. The pilot is fed with essential data from the radar and other systems on the head-up display in front of his eyes, so that he need not bring his attention inside the cockpit during combat. All essential controls are fitted on the throttle or sidestick controller, and this Hands On Throttle And Stick (HOTAS) system gives the pilot the best chance to use his armament of one 20-mm multi-barrel cannon and up to six Sidewinders to maximum effect. The Fighting Falcon is also a supreme attack aircraft with up to 12,000 lb (5,443 kg) of external

stores of all types. Like the F-15, the F-16 is being upgraded in power, electronics and armament on a continuous basis, the current F-16C being a match for any fighter in the world. The company has further plans for radical improvement, the most notable of these being a larger wing to restore wing loading to the original low figure (degraded by additional equipment and weapons) as a means of boosting agility. Another feature worth noting about the Eagle and Fighting Falcon (in common with other modern fighters) is the availability of two-seat versions for combat training. These two-seaters are generally comparable to the single-seaters in all essential respects, having the same combat capability though, in general, a slight reduction in fuel capacity to provide the volume for the larger cockpit and second seat.

The U.S.A.'s latest fighter is the McDonnell Douglas F/A-18 Hornet, a carrierborne type that has been adopted for the U.S. Navy and U.S. Marine Corps, and also sold to several export customers as a land-based machine. The Hornet first flew in 1978 after development and enlargement from Northrop's losing competitor in the Light-Weight Fighter competition won by the F-16. The Hornet marks a new departure in fighter design, as indicated by its official designation as a Fighter/Attack type with equal capability in each role. This has clear advantages for the carrierborne role, in which

the Hornet replaces the Phantom II fighter and Vought A-7 Corsair II attack aircraft as a single type with capabilities better than those of either of its predecessors. Given the Hornet's origins, it is not surprising that the F/A-18 is in some respects similar to the Fighting Falcon in possessing only moderately swept wings, comparatively unexceptional outright performance but excellent agility, acceleration and weapon-carrying capability. However the type has more power, in the form of two 16,000-lb (7,257-kg) afterburning thrust General Electric F404 turbofans, and provision for Sparrow as well as Sidewinder air-to-air missiles complementing the 20-mm multi-barrel cannon in the nose.

On the other side of the Atlantic comparable developments have been taking place to improve the front-line inventories of the U.S.S.R. and of the U.S.A.'s European allies. The new aircraft in the Soviet inventory stem from the two major design bureaux concerned with smaller military aircraft, namely Mikoyan-Gurevich and Sukhoi.

The former has been particularly prolific with a series of highly

Left: The General Dynamics F-16 is currently the 'last word' in fighter capability through its remarkable design and 'fly-by-wire' control system. The type has also proved remarkably adept in the attack role with a diversity of 'dumb' and 'smart' weapons.

Right: The Northrop F-17 was produced in competition to the F-16, but when it lost the 1974 fly-off against the F-16 was enlarged and developed, increasingly by the navally-experienced McDonnell Douglas, as the important F/A-18 Hornet carrierborne fighter and attack aircraft.

Below: The British Aerospace Sea Harrier FRS.Mk 1 is a naval development of the Harrier close-support aeroplane for the fighter, reconnaissance and strike roles. Additions include radar and more modern weapons, while a major design change is the raised cockpit and clear-view canopy for fighter-type fields of vision. The Sea Harrier proved decisive in the 1982 Falklands campaign against Argentina.

impressive aircraft in the 1960s, 1970s and 1980s. The first of these was a MiG-21 replacement in the air-combat role, namely the MiG-23, dubbed 'Flogger' by NATO. This is a capable type that first flew in 1967 on the power of a Tumansky R-27 afterburning turbojet, replaced on production machines by the 25,353-lb (11,500-kg) afterburning thrust R-29 from the same engine bureau. The most interesting feature of the MiG-23's design is the use of variable-geometry wings: contemporary Soviet 'swing-wing' types such as the Su-17 derivative of the Su-7 attack aircraft are characterised by hinged outer wing panels, but the MiG-23 has fully sweeping wings to provide the desired combination of high flight

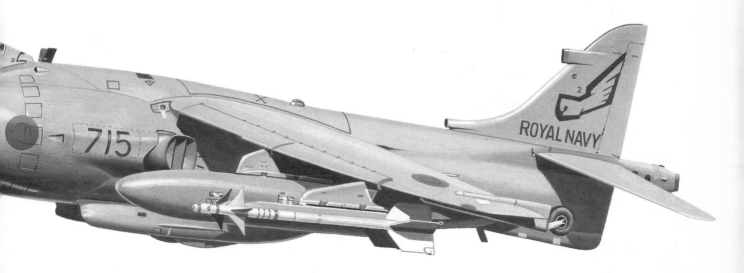

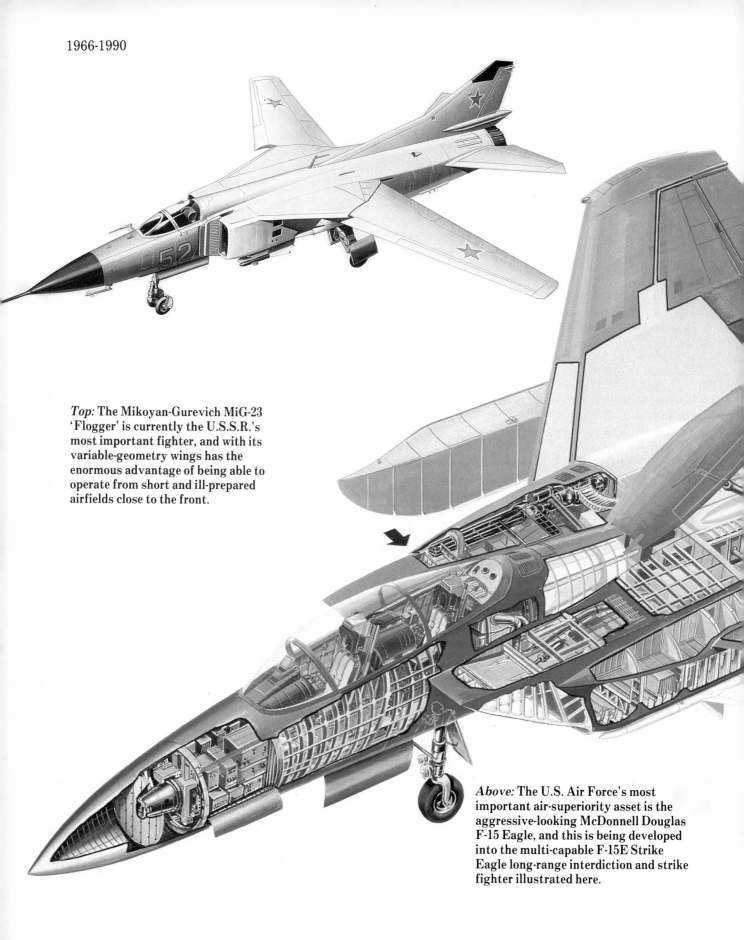

Top: The Mikoyan-Gurevich MiG-23 'Flogger' is currently the U.S.S.R.'s most important fighter, and with its variable-geometry wings has the enormous advantage of being able to operate from short and ill-prepared airfields close to the front.

Above: The U.S. Air Force's most important air-superiority asset is the aggressive-looking McDonnell Douglas F-15 Eagle, and this is being developed into the multi-capable F-15E Strike Eagle long-range interdiction and strike fighter illustrated here.

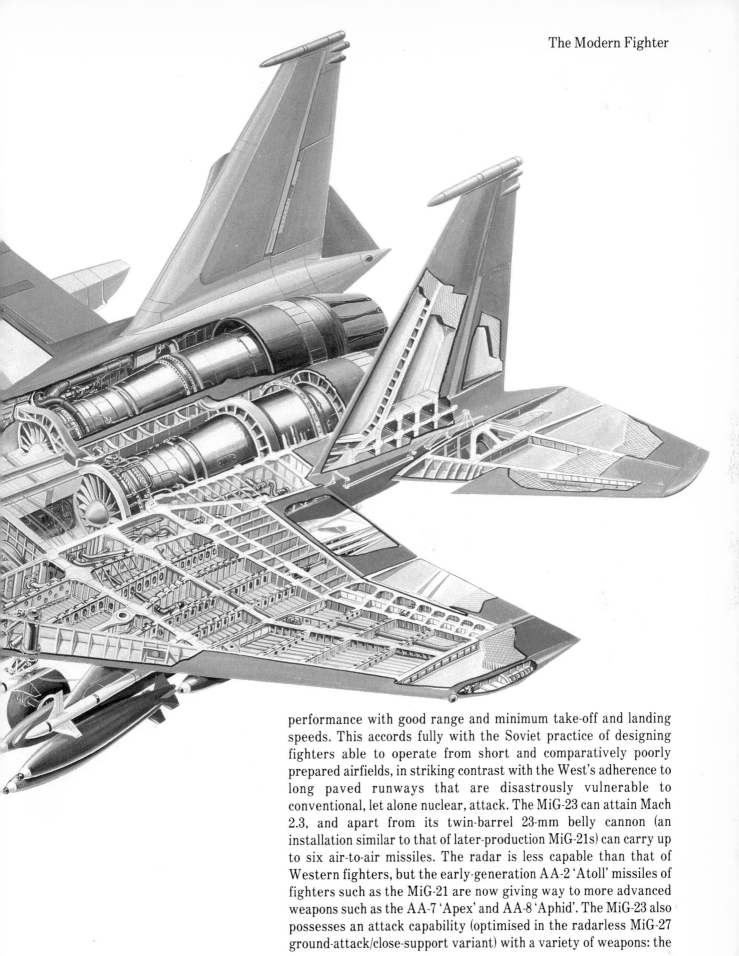

performance with good range and minimum take-off and landing speeds. This accords fully with the Soviet practice of designing fighters able to operate from short and comparatively poorly prepared airfields, in striking contrast with the West's adherence to long paved runways that are disastrously vulnerable to conventional, let alone nuclear, attack. The MiG-23 can attain Mach 2.3, and apart from its twin-barrel 23-mm belly cannon (an installation similar to that of later-production MiG-21s) can carry up to six air-to-air missiles. The radar is less capable than that of Western fighters, but the early-generation AA-2 'Atoll' missiles of fighters such as the MiG-21 are now giving way to more advanced weapons such as the AA-7 'Apex' and AA-8 'Aphid'. The MiG-23 also possesses an attack capability (optimised in the radarless MiG-27 ground-attack/close-support variant) with a variety of weapons: the

generally quoted figure of 6,616 lb (3,000 kg) for the MiG-23's disposable load is probably an underestimate of at least 2,205 lb (1,000 kg) and probably more.

The series has been developed through a number of variants, and has been exported to Soviet bloc countries and client states, the latter generally receiving a downgraded version with AA-2 missiles, 'Jay Bird' rather than the standard 'High Lark' radar, reducing search range from 53 miles (85 km) to 18 miles (29 km), and less capable electronic countermeasures.

Next in numerical sequence comes the MiG-25, dubbed 'Foxbat' by NATO. This air-defence interceptor was developed specifically to deal with the high-altitude strategic bomber being developed by the U.S.A. as the North American B-70 Valkyrie, but in the manner typical of Soviet procurement practices remained in development even after the B-70 had been cancelled. The type first flew in 1964 and has immense performance, with a maximum speed of Mach 2.8 attainable with four huge AA-6 'Acrid' air-to-air missiles on the power of two 27,116-lb (12,300-kg) afterburning thrust Tumansky R-31 turbojets. The radar is the heavy 'Fox Fire', which uses valve technology for the great 'burn-through' power required to secure target lock-on at a range of 56 miles (90 km) in conditions of electronic countermeasures. But for all this the 'Foxbat' is tactically

Left: **The Panavia Tornado was long in the gestation (a feature of multi-national programmes), but has matured as a quite exceptional aeroplane with the ability, in its Tornado IDS variant, to fly long distances at supersonic speed at very, very low level. Yet its thrust-reversing powerplant and swing wings allow the Tornado to operate from short runways or, perhaps more importantly, to use undamaged stretches of longer runways which have been subjected to conventional attack and cratered.**

Left: The Mikoyan-Gurevich MiG-29 'Fulcrum' is one of the latest Soviet fighters, and is clearly a formidable warplane, though little of a precise nature has been revealed about it.

Left: The Mikoyan-Gurevich MiG-31 'Foxhound' is a reworking of the MiG-25 'Foxbat' for better performance at medium altitudes and, more importantly, capability in radar and weapons for the detection and engagement of low-altitude targets.

limited: it is a high-altitude aircraft, and its capability to manoeuvre at its highest speeds is virtually nonexistent. The type has been developed as a useful strategic and operational reconnaissance aircraft, and in-service fighters have been updated to 'Foxbat-E' standard with more powerful engines, a pulse-Doppler radar more similar to that of American fighters, and thus capable of looking down for a target, and new AA-9 'Amos' long-range air-to-air missiles. The most likely targets for this version are cruise missiles and other low-level intruders.

The MiG-29 'Fulcrum' is an air-superiority and air-combat fighter closely similar to the F-16 in overall concept but in configuration similar to the F-15 and sized like the F/A-18. The type began to enter service in the mid-1980s, and is still little known in the West: it is powered by two 18,298-lb (8,300-kg) afterburning thrust Tumansky R-33 turbofans (one of the first such installations in the U.S.S.R.) for Mach 2.2 flight performance, has a capable pulse-Doppler radar, and carries as armament one 30-mm cannon and some six or eight air-to-air missiles.

Last in the numerical sequence, though produced somewhat

earlier than the MiG-29, the MiG-31 'Foxhound' is a radical reworking of the MiG-25 with a longer fuselage to accommodate a two-man crew, and optimised for lower-altitude interception with advanced missiles matched to a look-down radar of the pulse-Doppler type. The powerplant comprises two engines, probably 30,864-lb (14,000-kg) afterburning thrust Tumansky R-31F turbojets, and the MiG-31 can attain Mach 2.4 at altitude.

To partner the MiG-29 the Soviets have introduced the Sukhoi Su-27, dubbed 'Flanker' by NATO. This is similar in concept to the F-15, and began to enter service in the mid-1980s. The type has Mach 2.35 performance on the power of two turbofans of unknown type, each rated at a probable afterburning thrust of about 29,982 lb (13,600 kg), and carries a capable pulse-Doppler radar with a search range of 149 miles (240 km). It is claimed that this radar relies heavily on technology 'gleaned' from the West, and certainly there has been a quantum improvement in Soviet radar capability within a very short time. The radar is matched to a fit of up to eight air-to-air missiles, including the new AA-10 'Alamo', and the fighter is also fitted with a powerful multi-barrel cannon, probably of 30-mm

Top and above: **Though cancelled by a hard-pressed government in 1987, the IAI Lavi was a fascinating multi-role fighter, with American financial and technical support, to provide the Israeli Air Force with a warplane to succeed several other aircraft in roles as diverse as air combat, interdiction and close support.**

calibre. The 'Flanker' can also be used in the attack role, probably with a maximum of 13,228 lb (6,000 kg) of disposable stores.

Though nothing has been revealed publicly in the Western literature, it is certain that the U.S.S.R. is also working towards a new generation of fighters, using the latest aerodynamic concepts, electronic developments, and advanced composite materials in their structures, paralleling Western programmes such as the Advanced Tactical Fighter in the U.S.A., the EFA-90 (European Fighter Aircraft for the 1990s) in the U.K., West Germany, Italy and Spain, the Dassault-Breguet Rafale (squall) in France, and the Saab JAS 39 Gripen (griffon) in Sweden. In overall concept the emphasis is placed on versatility, and also on agility rather than outright performance, though of course advanced radars and other electronic features will be the norm for these highly agile small aircraft.

These new-generation fighters are due to enter service in the 1990s, and the current European fighters are thus the single-seat Dassault-Breguet Mirage 2000, the single-seat British Aerospace Sea Harrier FRS.Mk 1, the two-seat Panavia Tornado ADV and the single-seat Saab JA 37 Viggen (thunderbolt). The Mirage 2000 is an air-superiority fighter used by France and a number of export customers. In layout the Mirage 2000 is a reworking of the Mirage III concept: but whereas the Mirage III was an indifferent performer in turning engagements, losing energy rapidly because of its large delta wing, the Mirage 2000 uses the combination of 'fly-by-wire' control technology and leading/trailing-edge surfaces for Mach 2.2 performance and sustained agility. Power is provided by a 19,840-lb (9,000-kg) afterburning thrust SNECMA M53 bleed-turbojet (essentially a turbofan), and a capable look-down radar of the pulse-Doppler type allows the use of the up to three Super 530

Right: **An overhead view of the Grumman F-14 Tomcat emphasises the salient design features of this potent fighter, including the huge blended fuselage/powerplant, the twin vertical tail surfaces, and the large wings which, when swept fully aft, give the Tomcat virtually a delta configuration in association with the close-coupled tailplane.**

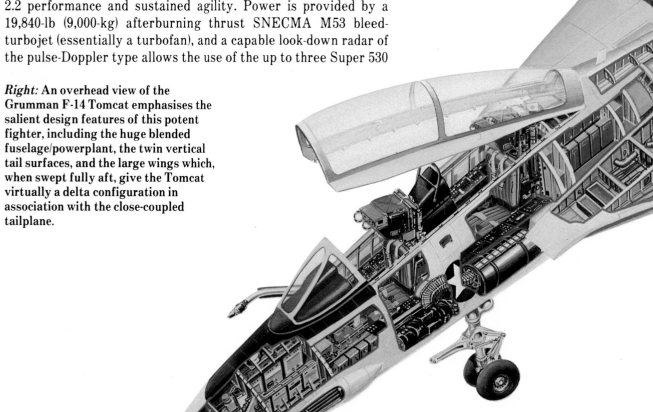

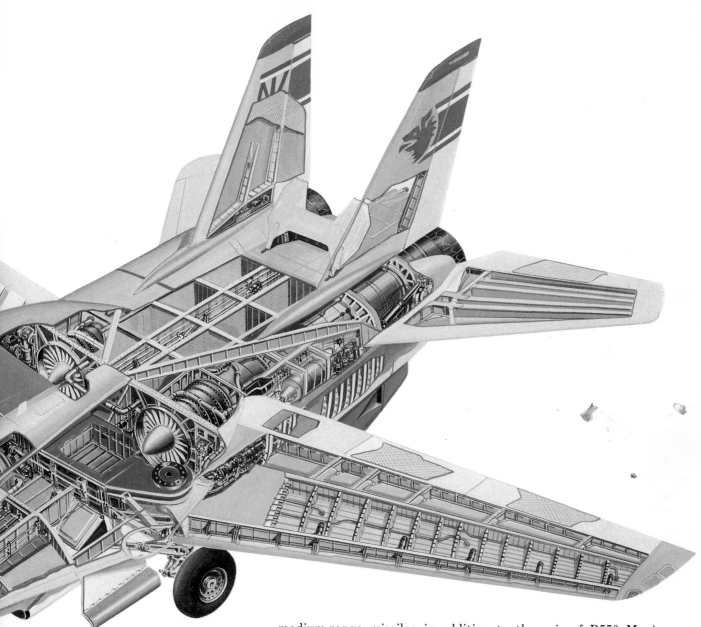

medium-range missiles in addition to the pair of R550 Magic dogfighting missiles and two 30-mm cannon. In the attack role, where it performs indifferently at low altitude, the Mirage 2000 can lift 13,889 lb (6,300 kg) of disposable stores.

Derived from the Harrier land-based close-support aeroplane, the Sea Harrier is a unique carrierborne multi-role fighter with reconnaissance and attack/strike capabilities. The Harrier was by no means designed for air combat, but in a number of trials showed that it could use its engine's thrust-vectoring system (designed, of course, to give the type a vertical take-off and landing capability) to achieve totally unrivalled aerial agility: the trials confirmed that the Harrier could outmanoeuvre even dedicated air-combat fighters to evade attack and usually get onto the tail of the attacker. So when the small carriers of the 'Invincible' class were mooted for the Royal Navy, it was logical to evolve a dedicated multi-role fighter

Left: The Dassault-Breguet Rafale (squall) is being developed in landplane and carrierborne variants for service with the French forces in the 1990s. In common with the new generation of fighters, the Rafale makes extensive use of composite materials in its structure, and is based on a canard configuration for maximum agility and effective control at high angles of attack.

Below: Pioneer of the modern canard fighter, the Saab 37 Viggen is a large but highly capable aeroplane with excellent performance married to a genuine STOL (Short Take-Off and Landing) capability to allow operations from short stretches of road.

derivative of the Harrier as the Sea Harrier, which began to enter service in 1981. The Sea Harrier has a Rolls-Royce Pegasus Mk 104 vectoring turbofan rated at 21,500-lb (9,752-kg) thrust, a revised nose section with the cockpit located higher under a bubble canopy, and Ferranti Blue Fox multi-mode pulse-Doppler radar. The armament comprises a pair of 30-mm cannon in pods under the fuselage (where they help trap exhaust gas in the hover and so promote lift) and two or four Sidewinder missiles. The original Sea Harrier FRS.Mk 1 is to be supplanted by the FRS.Mk 2 with the more capable Blue Vixen radar matched to AMRAAM missiles in addition to the original Sidewinders. Up to 8,000 lb (3,629 kg) of disposable stores can be carried.

The Tornado Air-Defence Variant is a British development of the multi-national Tornado IDS two-seat long-range interdiction and strike aircraft. This first flew in 1974, and is the West's premier low-level attack and strike aircraft through its excellent variable-geometry design and two economical Turbo-Union RB.199 turbofans, each rated at 16,800-lb (7,620-kg) afterburning thrust. The Tornado ADV has greater power, a lengthened fuselage to accommodate four BAe Sky Flash missiles semi-recessed under the fuselage, and Ferranti Foxhunter radar in the nose. The radar is potentially a formidable look-down unit with great search range, but has been plagued by development problems. But once these problems have been eradicated, the Tornado ADV will be a potent Mach 2.2 air-superiority fighter, with usefully improved acceleration and range thanks to the reduced drag and increased fuel capacity of the longer fuselage.

Above: The British Aerospace EAP was produced as a flying testbed for a host of the latest aerodynamic, electronic and structural features, and is now being used as a testbed towards the development of the multi-national European Fighter Aircraft.

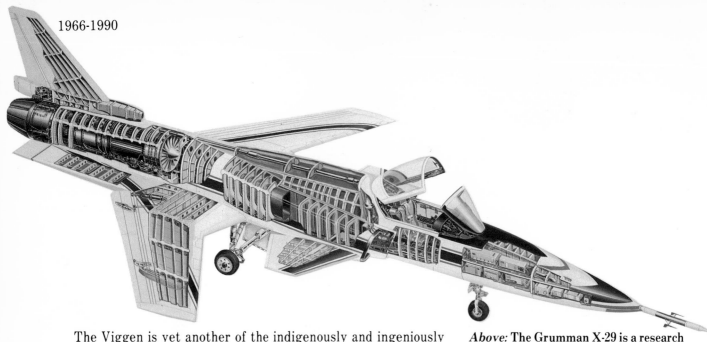

The Viggen is yet another of the indigenously and ingeniously designed Swedish fighters which have proved that given the will, even a comparatively small country can develop a combat aeroplane the match for anything else in the world. The Viggen was developed in the 1960s (first flying in 1967) as the aeroplane component of a complete weapons system including the air-defence network and ground installations. The type was first produced in attack, reconnaissance and trainer variants, and only finally as the JA 37 interceptor with the 28,108-lb (12,750-kg) afterburning thrust Volvo Flygmotor RM8B turbofan, a licence-built derivative of the Pratt & Whitney JT8D civil turbofan fitted with a Swedish-designed afterburner. The engine is part of the key to the Viggen's capability, the other two being the advanced Ericsson pulse-Doppler radar (together with four Sky Flash missiles) and the aeroplane's radical aerodynamics. It is an essential part of Sweden's defence posture that combat operations be undertaken from dispersed sites (roads etc.) not prone to wholesale destruction in a pre-emptive attack, and the Viggen thus needs STOL field performance: this was provided by the use of a large essentially delta wing married to a small canard wing to provide precise control at low speeds and high angles of attack. The Viggen can thus be flown rather than drifted onto the runway, an automatic system ensuring that the brakes and thrust reverser are engaged the moment the nosewheel leg is compressed. The Viggen can also carry Sidewinder short-range missiles, and is fitted with one Oerlikon-Bührle KCA cannon, a 30-mm weapon firing heavy shells with a muzzle velocity so high that their trajectory is almost flat, and thus fairly simple to aim.

Thus the fighter is still very much with us, and likely to remain so in the years to come. Allowing for the enormous changes in technology since the fighter first appeared in 1915, the role of this important type has altered very little: its primary task is still the destruction of the enemy's aircraft, and if other roles have been grafted onto this primary task, it is surely a recognition of the fighter's technical and tactical predominance over other combat aircraft.

Above: The Grumman X-29 is a research aeroplane rather than fighter, but its swept-forward wings and canard foreplanes are being evaluated as a combination that may well appear on fighters of the future.

Below: The Saab JAS 39 Gripen is intended to succeed the Viggen, and it is interesting to note how technological developments, especially in aerodynamics, electronics, engines and structures has made possible a considerably smaller design that sacrifices nothing in capability to its illustrious forebear.

INDEX

References to illustrations are in *italic*.

160